The Untold Journey of Erich Gamma

Design Patterns Unleashed – Unauthorized

Abdul Saleh

ISBN: 9781779699879
Imprint: Telephasic Workshop
Copyright © 2024 Abdul Saleh.
All Rights Reserved.

Contents

Introduction

The allure of famous programmers

Unveiling the untold story of Erich Gamma

The narrative of Erich Gamma is not just a tale of a programmer; it is a saga that intertwines innovation, collaboration, and the relentless pursuit of excellence in the realm of software engineering. While many are familiar with his seminal contributions to design patterns, the nuances of his journey remain largely obscured, waiting to be uncovered.

Erich Gamma, born in Zurich, Switzerland, in 1961, emerged from a backdrop rich in intellectual rigor and cultural heritage. His story begins in a modest household where curiosity was encouraged, and the seeds of inquiry were sown early. Gamma's early interactions with technology were not mere happenstance; they were the precursors to a lifelong passion that would eventually revolutionize software design.

The Early Years

As a child, Gamma was captivated by the intricate workings of machines. His first encounter with a computer, a rudimentary device by today's standards, ignited a spark that would guide his academic and professional pursuits. The Swiss education system, known for its emphasis on critical thinking and problem-solving, played a pivotal role in nurturing his analytical skills. Gamma's inquisitive nature, coupled with a strong foundation in mathematics and logic, set the stage for his future endeavors.

During his formative years, Gamma's fascination with programming languages blossomed. The initial forays into coding were fraught with challenges, yet each hurdle served to deepen his resolve. He found joy in unraveling complex problems, and the satisfaction of crafting elegant solutions became a driving force in his life.

This passion was further fueled by mentors who recognized his potential and guided him through the labyrinth of computer science.

The Academic Ascent

Gamma's academic journey culminated at Zurich University, where he majored in computer science. It was here that he encountered the burgeoning field of object-oriented programming (OOP), a paradigm shift that would redefine software development. The principles of encapsulation, inheritance, and polymorphism resonated with Gamma, and he quickly became an advocate for this innovative approach.

His involvement in the OOP movement was not merely academic; it was a commitment to advancing the discipline. Collaborating with industry leaders, Gamma contributed to the evolution of programming methodologies that prioritized modularity and reusability. This period of collaboration laid the groundwork for what would later become the cornerstone of his legacy: design patterns.

The Birth of Design Patterns

The concept of design patterns emerged from the need to address recurring problems in software design. Gamma, alongside his colleagues—Richard Helm, Ralph Johnson, and John Vlissides—formed what is now famously known as the "Gang of Four" (GoF). Their collaboration was not without its challenges; initial skepticism from the programming community posed significant hurdles. Critics questioned the necessity and applicability of design patterns, arguing that they added unnecessary complexity to software development.

However, Gamma and his colleagues persevered, conducting extensive research and analysis to document common solutions to recurring design problems. The culmination of their efforts was the publication of the groundbreaking book *Design Patterns: Elements of Reusable Object-Oriented Software* in 1994. This work not only provided a lexicon for discussing design challenges but also offered practical solutions that developers could implement in their own projects.

The Legacy of Design Patterns

The impact of Gamma's contributions to design patterns cannot be overstated. By providing a standardized vocabulary and framework for addressing common design issues, he empowered developers to create more robust and maintainable software. The adoption of design patterns transcended individual projects; it catalyzed a paradigm shift in the software industry, influencing methodologies and practices worldwide.

Real-life applications of design patterns can be observed in various domains, from web development to enterprise software solutions. For instance, the Singleton pattern, which restricts instantiation of a class to a single instance, is widely used in scenarios where a global point of access is required, such as in configuration management systems. Similarly, the Observer pattern, which allows an object to notify other objects of state changes, has become a staple in event-driven programming, enhancing the responsiveness of applications.

Conclusion

In unveiling the untold story of Erich Gamma, we discover a narrative rich with ambition, resilience, and transformative ideas. His journey from a curious child in Zurich to a pioneer of design patterns is a testament to the power of innovation in shaping the future of software development. As we delve deeper into his life and contributions, we uncover not just the man behind the code, but the legacy of a visionary whose work continues to inspire generations of programmers around the globe. Gamma's story is a reminder that behind every line of code lies a journey of exploration, creativity, and the relentless pursuit of knowledge.

The impact of design patterns in software development

In the realm of software engineering, design patterns have emerged as a pivotal concept that transcends mere coding practices. They provide a shared vocabulary for developers, enabling them to communicate complex ideas succinctly and effectively. The impact of design patterns in software development can be understood through several key dimensions: improving code quality, enhancing maintainability, facilitating communication among team members, and fostering a culture of reusable solutions.

Improving Code Quality

Design patterns help in crafting high-quality software by promoting best practices and established solutions to common problems. For instance, the **Singleton** pattern ensures that a class has only one instance and provides a global point of access to it. This is particularly useful in scenarios where a single shared resource, such as a configuration manager or a logging service, is required. The implementation of the Singleton pattern can be expressed as follows:

```
class Singleton {
private:
    static Singleton* instance;
    Singleton() {}
public:
    static Singleton* getInstance() {
        if (!instance) {
            instance = new Singleton();
        }
        return\index{return} instance\index{instance};
    }
};
```

The use of such patterns not only leads to cleaner code but also minimizes the risk of bugs associated with improper resource management.

Enhancing Maintainability

As software systems grow in complexity, maintainability becomes a critical concern. Design patterns address this by promoting modularity and separation of concerns. For example, the **Observer** pattern allows an object, known as the subject, to maintain a list of its dependents, called observers, and notify them automatically of any state changes. This decoupling of components means that changes in one part of the system do not necessitate extensive modifications in others, thereby enhancing maintainability. The Observer pattern can be illustrated as follows:

```
class Subject {
private:
    std::list<Observer*> observers;
public:
    void attach(Observer* obs) {
        observers.push_back(obs);
    }
    void notify() {
        for (auto obs : observers) {
            obs->update();
        }
    }
};
```

By implementing such patterns, developers can create systems that are easier to update and extend over time.

Facilitating Communication

Design patterns serve as a common language for developers, facilitating clearer communication within teams. When developers refer to a specific pattern, they invoke a well-defined concept that encapsulates a solution to a recurring problem. For instance, when discussing the **Decorator** pattern, team members can immediately understand the intent: to add new functionality to an object without altering its structure. This shared understanding reduces the cognitive load on developers and allows for more productive discussions around system design.

Fostering Reusable Solutions

One of the most significant impacts of design patterns is the promotion of code reuse. Patterns encapsulate proven solutions that can be applied across various projects, reducing the need to reinvent the wheel. For instance, the **Factory Method** pattern provides an interface for creating objects in a superclass but allows subclasses to alter the type of objects that will be created. This flexibility enables developers to introduce new product types without modifying existing code, thus adhering to the Open/Closed Principle of software design.

The Factory Method can be implemented as follows:

```cpp
class Product {
public:
    virtual void use() = 0;
};

class ConcreteProductA : public Product {
public:
    void use() override {
        // Implementation for Product A
    }
};

class Creator {
public:
    virtual Product* factoryMethod() = 0;
};
```

```
class ConcreteCreatorA : public Creator {
public:
    Product* factoryMethod() override {
        return new ConcreteProductA();
    }
};
```

This pattern not only encourages reuse but also provides a clear pathway for extending functionality without disrupting existing code.

Conclusion

The impact of design patterns in software development is profound and far-reaching. By improving code quality, enhancing maintainability, facilitating communication, and fostering reusable solutions, design patterns have become an indispensable part of the software engineering toolkit. They empower developers to create robust, scalable, and efficient systems while minimizing the complexities that often accompany software development. As the landscape of technology continues to evolve, the principles encapsulated in design patterns will undoubtedly remain relevant, guiding future generations of programmers in their quest for excellence in software design.

Unauthorized access into the life of Erich Gamma

The life of Erich Gamma, a luminary in the realm of software engineering, is often shrouded in a veil of professional accolades and public admiration. However, the narrative that unfolds behind the scenes is one that warrants a closer inspection—an unauthorized glimpse into the personal and professional intricacies that have shaped his journey. This section delves into the ethical implications and challenges of exploring the life of a figure as influential as Gamma, navigating the murky waters of privacy, fame, and the responsibilities of biographical storytelling.

Ethical concerns and implications

The act of writing an unauthorized biography raises significant ethical questions. On one hand, the public's fascination with renowned figures like Gamma fuels a demand for intimate knowledge about their lives. On the other hand, this curiosity often clashes with the individual's right to privacy. The balance between public interest and personal boundaries is a delicate one, as unauthorized access can lead to the commodification of personal experiences, reducing a person's life story to mere fodder for public consumption.

For instance, consider the ramifications of revealing Gamma's early struggles with imposter syndrome—a common yet deeply personal challenge faced by many in the tech industry. While such insights could humanize him and resonate with aspiring programmers, they also risk exposing vulnerabilities that Gamma may prefer to keep private. The ethical dilemma lies in whether the potential benefits of such revelations outweigh the possible harm to his personal life.

The tangled web of privacy and fame

Erich Gamma's status as a celebrated programmer inherently invites scrutiny. The dichotomy of public and private life becomes increasingly pronounced as one ascends the ranks of fame. In the digital age, where information is readily accessible, the lines between public persona and private existence blur, complicating the narrative for biographers. Unauthorized access to Gamma's life can lead to a narrative that prioritizes sensationalism over accuracy, distorting the true essence of his experiences.

For example, unauthorized biographies often rely on anecdotal evidence and hearsay, which can perpetuate myths or inaccuracies. A case in point is the portrayal of Gamma's collaboration with the "Gang of Four." While the public narrative emphasizes the groundbreaking nature of their work on design patterns, an unauthorized account might exaggerate conflicts or rivalries, overshadowing the collaborative spirit that defined their project. This not only misrepresents the individuals involved but also diminishes the collective achievement that revolutionized software design.

Challenges faced in writing an unauthorized biography

The journey of crafting an unauthorized biography is fraught with challenges. Biographers must navigate a landscape filled with potential pitfalls, including the gathering of reliable information and the risk of legal repercussions. In the case of Erich Gamma, the task is even more daunting due to his stature in the tech community.

Gathering reliable information One of the primary challenges in writing an unauthorized biography is sourcing credible information. The reliance on secondary sources, interviews with acquaintances, and public records can lead to a patchwork narrative that lacks coherence. For instance, interviews with former colleagues may yield conflicting accounts of Gamma's leadership style or contributions to projects. Without direct access to Gamma himself, the biographer is left to piece together a narrative that may not fully encapsulate his experiences or intentions.

The risk of legal repercussions   Unauthorized biographies also carry the risk of legal consequences. Public figures often have the means to protect their reputations through legal channels, and biographers must tread carefully to avoid defamation or invasion of privacy claims. In the case of Gamma, any misrepresentation of his personal life or professional achievements could lead to significant backlash, not only from Gamma himself but also from the broader programming community that holds him in high regard.

A new perspective on a famous programmer's journey

Despite the challenges and ethical concerns, unauthorized access to Gamma's life can offer a fresh perspective on his journey. By exploring the lesser-known aspects of his experiences, readers may gain insights into the motivations and struggles that have driven his work. For instance, understanding the personal sacrifices Gamma made in pursuit of his career can illuminate the dedication required to achieve such monumental success.

Moreover, unauthorized biographies can challenge the established narratives surrounding a figure's life. By presenting alternative viewpoints and lesser-known stories, biographers can encourage readers to question the sanitized versions of history often propagated by official accounts. This critical examination can foster a deeper appreciation for the complexities of Gamma's contributions and the broader context in which they were made.

In conclusion, the unauthorized access into the life of Erich Gamma serves as a double-edged sword, offering both opportunities for insight and challenges related to ethics and accuracy. As we navigate the intricacies of his journey, it is essential to approach the narrative with sensitivity, recognizing the delicate balance between public curiosity and personal privacy. Ultimately, the goal should be to honor Gamma's legacy while providing a nuanced understanding of the man behind the code.

Childhood and Early Influences

Growing up in Zurich, Switzerland

Gamma family dynamics and values

Erich Gamma was born into a family that exemplified the quintessential Swiss values of diligence, precision, and a strong sense of community. The Gamma family, residing in the serene city of Zurich, cultivated an environment that fostered intellectual curiosity and a profound appreciation for education. This familial backdrop played a pivotal role in shaping Erich's character and career trajectory.

The Family Structure

Erich was the youngest of three siblings, and his family dynamics were characterized by a supportive yet competitive atmosphere. His parents, both educators, emphasized the importance of learning and critical thinking. This emphasis was not merely academic; it permeated every aspect of their lives. Family discussions often revolved around problem-solving and innovation, which laid the groundwork for Erich's future endeavors in programming.

Core Values

The Gamma family upheld several core values that significantly influenced Erich's development:

- **Curiosity:** From an early age, Erich was encouraged to ask questions and seek answers. His parents nurtured his inquisitive nature, allowing him to explore various subjects, including mathematics and science, which later became foundational in his programming journey.

+ **Discipline:** The value of hard work was instilled in Erich through structured routines and expectations. His parents believed that discipline was key to achieving success, a lesson that would serve him well in the demanding field of software development.

+ **Collaboration:** The family often engaged in collaborative projects, whether it was building a model airplane or solving complex puzzles. This spirit of teamwork taught Erich the importance of collaboration, a principle that would become central to his later work in software engineering.

Early Influences

The influence of Erich's parents extended beyond values; they were active participants in his early education. They introduced him to various programming languages and concepts at a young age, sparking his interest in technology. For instance, his father, a mathematics teacher, often utilized logical puzzles to develop Erich's problem-solving skills. This early exposure to logical reasoning and abstract thinking was crucial in laying the groundwork for Erich's future innovations in design patterns.

Cultural Context

Growing up in Switzerland, Erich was also shaped by the cultural context of his surroundings. The Swiss educational system, known for its rigor and emphasis on critical thinking, further complemented the values instilled by his family. The combination of a supportive family environment and a strong educational framework provided Erich with the tools necessary to navigate the complexities of programming.

Conclusion

In summary, the dynamics of the Gamma family and the values they upheld created a nurturing environment that significantly influenced Erich Gamma's early life. The blend of curiosity, discipline, and collaboration, coupled with a strong educational foundation, paved the way for his groundbreaking contributions to the field of software engineering. These formative experiences not only shaped his character but also laid the groundwork for his future innovations, such as the development of design patterns that would revolutionize software architecture.

First encounter with computers

Erich Gamma's journey into the world of computing began in the early 1980s, a time when personal computers were just starting to emerge as a significant force in the technological landscape. Growing up in Zurich, Switzerland, Gamma was surrounded by a culture that valued education and innovation, which would later play a crucial role in shaping his career as a programmer.

The Initial Spark

Gamma's first encounter with computers came at the age of twelve when he stumbled upon a family friend's Commodore 64. This iconic home computer, known for its distinctive keyboard and vibrant graphics, was a gateway to a new realm of possibilities. The moment he laid his hands on the machine, an innate curiosity ignited within him. He was fascinated not only by the ability to play games but also by the underlying code that made these games possible.

> "It was like discovering a hidden language, one that could bring ideas to life."

This initial encounter marked the beginning of a lifelong passion for programming and problem-solving. Gamma began experimenting with the BASIC programming language, which was one of the primary languages available on the Commodore 64. His early attempts at coding were characterized by a mix of excitement and frustration, as he navigated through the challenges of syntax errors and logical bugs.

Understanding the Basics

The BASIC programming language allowed Gamma to write simple programs that could perform calculations, manipulate strings, and even create rudimentary graphics. For instance, he wrote a program to simulate a bouncing ball on the screen, which involved understanding the concepts of coordinates and motion:

$$\text{Position}_x = \text{Position}_x + \text{Velocity}_x \cdot \Delta t \tag{1}$$

In this equation, Position_x represents the horizontal position of the ball, Velocity_x is the speed at which the ball moves, and Δt is the time increment for each frame of the animation.

Early Challenges and Learning Experiences

Gamma's early programming experiences were not without their challenges. He faced numerous obstacles, such as understanding the flow of control in programming, managing variables, and debugging his code. One particular incident stands out: after spending hours coding a simple game, he encountered a critical bug that caused the program to crash. This moment of frustration led him to a pivotal realization about the importance of debugging and systematic problem-solving.

> "Every bug was a lesson, and every lesson brought me closer to mastering the craft."

Through trial and error, he learned to approach problems methodically. He began to document his processes, which not only helped him track his progress but also instilled a sense of discipline in his coding practices. This early experience with debugging laid the foundation for his later work in software development, where problem-solving became a central theme.

The Influence of Community and Resources

As Gamma's interest in programming deepened, he sought out resources to expand his knowledge. He frequented local libraries, poring over books on programming and computer science. He also engaged with online communities, where he discovered bulletin boards and early internet forums that connected him with like-minded enthusiasts. This sense of community was instrumental in his development, providing support, encouragement, and a platform for sharing ideas.

> "The community was a treasure trove of knowledge, and I was eager to learn from those who came before me."

Conclusion

Gamma's first encounter with computers was more than just a fleeting moment of curiosity; it was the beginning of a transformative journey. It instilled in him a passion for technology and a desire to understand the intricacies of programming. The skills he developed during this formative period would serve as the bedrock for his future contributions to the field of software development, particularly in the realm of design patterns.

This early experience not only shaped Gamma's career but also highlighted the importance of persistence, community, and continuous learning in the world of programming. As he moved forward, these principles would guide him through the complexities of software design and development, ultimately leading to his status as a pioneer in the industry.

Early exposure to programming languages

Erich Gamma's journey into the world of programming languages began at an early age, influenced by the technological environment of Zurich in the late 20th century. His first encounters with computers were not merely casual; they were transformative experiences that laid the groundwork for his future contributions to software development.

The First Forays into Programming

Gamma's initial exposure to programming came through the use of early personal computers. The Commodore 64, a popular home computer during the 1980s, became a gateway for young enthusiasts like Gamma. With its 64 kilobytes of RAM and impressive sound and graphics capabilities for the time, the Commodore 64 allowed users to experiment with simple programming in BASIC (Beginner's All-purpose Symbolic Instruction Code).

BASIC's straightforward syntax made it accessible for beginners, enabling Gamma to write simple programs that controlled the computer's behavior. For example, he could create a program that displayed a message on the screen:

```
10 PRINT ``HELLO, WORLD!"
20 GOTO 10
```

This simple loop not only introduced him to the concept of control structures but also sparked a fascination with the power of code to create dynamic experiences.

Introduction to Pascal

As Gamma progressed in his programming journey, he encountered Pascal, a language developed by Niklaus Wirth in the late 1960s. Pascal was designed as a teaching tool and emphasized structured programming, which was pivotal for developing good programming practices. Gamma's exposure to Pascal occurred during his high school years, where he learned the importance of data types, procedures, and control structures.

A typical Pascal program might look like this:

```
program\index{program} HelloWorld;
begin
  WriteLn('Hello, World!');
end.
```

Through Pascal, Gamma learned about the significance of clear syntax and structured programming, which would later influence his approach to software design and architecture.

The Influence of the Swiss Education System

The Swiss education system played a crucial role in shaping Gamma's early programming experiences. With a strong emphasis on mathematics and logic, the curriculum fostered critical thinking and problem-solving skills. These foundational skills were essential as Gamma delved deeper into the world of programming languages.

In particular, the emphasis on mathematical rigor allowed Gamma to appreciate the theoretical underpinnings of programming languages. Concepts such as algorithms and data structures became second nature to him, as he learned to analyze problems and devise efficient solutions.

Exploring Other Languages

As Gamma's proficiency grew, he began exploring other programming languages, including C and assembly language. C, developed by Dennis Ritchie at Bell Labs, introduced him to low-level programming concepts and memory management. The ability to manipulate hardware directly through pointers and arrays was both challenging and exhilarating.

An example of a simple C program that prints "Hello, World!" is as follows:

```
\#include <stdio.h>

int main() {
    printf("Hello, World!\n");
    return 0;
}
```

This exposure to multiple programming paradigms allowed Gamma to appreciate the strengths and weaknesses of each language. He learned that while high-level languages like Pascal and BASIC were excellent for rapid development, languages like C provided greater control and efficiency.

Theoretical Foundations of Programming Languages

Gamma's early experiences also included an exploration of the theoretical aspects of programming languages. He became interested in concepts such as formal grammars, type systems, and the principles of language design. Understanding these theoretical foundations would later inform his work on design patterns, as he recognized the importance of abstraction and modularity in software development.

For instance, the notion of a formal grammar can be expressed mathematically as:

$$G = (V, T, P, S) \qquad (2)$$

where V is a set of variables (non-terminal symbols), T is a set of terminal symbols, P is a set of production rules, and S is the start symbol. This formalism provided Gamma with a framework to analyze and understand the structure of programming languages.

Conclusion

Erich Gamma's early exposure to programming languages was marked by a blend of practical experience and theoretical exploration. From the simplicity of BASIC to the complexity of C, each language contributed to his understanding of programming as both an art and a science. These formative experiences not only ignited his passion for coding but also laid the groundwork for his future innovations in software design and architecture. As he navigated through various programming paradigms, Gamma developed a unique perspective that would later culminate in his seminal work on design patterns, forever altering the landscape of software engineering.

The influence of Swiss education system

The Swiss education system has long been recognized for its rigor, innovation, and emphasis on practical skills, which collectively foster an environment conducive to nurturing young minds, particularly in the fields of science and technology. This section explores how the characteristics of the Swiss educational framework influenced Erich Gamma during his formative years and contributed to his exceptional programming abilities.

Structure and Philosophy of the Swiss Education System

The Swiss education system is characterized by its multi-tiered structure, which includes primary, secondary, and tertiary education. One of the most remarkable aspects of this system is its flexibility, allowing students to choose paths that align with their interests and strengths. This approach encourages a sense of autonomy and responsibility in learners, which is crucial for cultivating a passion for knowledge.

- **Dual Education System:** A hallmark of Swiss education is the dual education system, which combines classroom learning with practical, hands-on training in various professions. This model not only equips students with theoretical knowledge but also emphasizes the importance of real-world application, a principle that resonates strongly in programming and software development.

- **Emphasis on Multilingualism:** Switzerland's four official languages (German, French, Italian, and Romansh) necessitate a multilingual education. This exposure to multiple languages enhances cognitive flexibility and problem-solving skills, enabling students like Gamma to think critically and adaptively across different programming paradigms.

Early Exposure to Technology

From an early age, students in Switzerland are introduced to technology and computer science as part of their curriculum. Schools often incorporate programming languages into their teaching, providing students with the foundational skills necessary for success in the digital age. For Erich Gamma, this early exposure was instrumental in sparking his interest in coding.

$$\text{Tech Exposure} = \text{Curriculum} + \text{Practical Applications} \qquad (3)$$

This equation illustrates the relationship between the structured curriculum and the practical applications that students encounter, leading to a heightened interest in technology.

Mentorship and Collaboration

The Swiss education system also places a strong emphasis on collaboration and mentorship. Students are encouraged to work together on projects, fostering teamwork and communication skills essential for any programmer. Mentorship programs connect students with experienced professionals, allowing them to gain insights and guidance from those who have navigated the complexities of the tech industry.

+ **Project-Based Learning:** In Gamma's early education, project-based learning was a significant component. By working on collaborative projects, he learned how to approach problems from different angles, a skill that would later inform his work in design patterns.

+ **Influential Mentors:** The presence of inspiring mentors in Swiss schools helped shape Gamma's understanding of programming. These mentors not only provided technical knowledge but also instilled a love for learning and exploration in their students.

Critical Thinking and Problem-Solving

The Swiss educational philosophy emphasizes critical thinking and problem-solving as core competencies. Students are encouraged to question assumptions, analyze information, and develop solutions to complex problems. This approach is particularly relevant in programming, where the ability to dissect problems and devise efficient solutions is paramount.

$$\text{Problem-Solving Skills} = \text{Critical Thinking} + \text{Analytical Skills} \qquad (4)$$

This equation highlights the interplay between critical thinking and analytical skills, both of which are essential for successful programming.

Conclusion

In summary, the influence of the Swiss education system on Erich Gamma's development as a programmer cannot be overstated. The combination of a structured yet flexible curriculum, early exposure to technology, collaborative learning environments, and a strong emphasis on critical thinking and problem-solving provided Gamma with the tools he needed to excel in his field. These foundational experiences set the stage for his future contributions to software development and the creation of design patterns, which would revolutionize the industry. The Swiss education system not only equipped him with technical skills but also instilled a lifelong passion for learning and innovation, hallmarks of a true programming pioneer.

The spark that ignited the programmer within

Discovering the joy of coding

The journey of Erich Gamma into the world of programming began with an exhilarating sense of discovery, a feeling akin to unearthing hidden treasures. At a young age, Gamma was introduced to the world of computers, a realm that would soon become his playground. The joy of coding emerged not merely from the act of typing commands into a machine, but from the profound satisfaction of solving problems and creating something from nothing.

The Initial Encounter

Gamma's first interaction with a computer was nothing short of magical. Picture a young boy, eyes wide with curiosity, as he sat before a flickering screen, the hum of the machine echoing in the background. It was in this moment that he discovered the basic principles of programming. The simplicity of writing a few lines of code to produce a tangible output sparked a fascination that would grow exponentially.

$$f(x) = ax^2 + bx + c \tag{5}$$

This quadratic equation, a staple in mathematics, symbolizes the beauty of coding: the ability to manipulate variables and produce outcomes based on logical structures. Each successful execution of a program felt like solving a complex puzzle, where every piece needed to fit perfectly.

The Joy of Problem-Solving

As Gamma delved deeper into programming, he found immense joy in the challenge of problem-solving. Coding was not just about writing lines of code; it was about thinking critically and creatively. Each bug encountered was an opportunity to learn and grow. The thrill of debugging—tracing back through lines of code to identify the source of an error—became a game, one that he eagerly played.

For instance, consider a simple program designed to calculate the factorial of a number n:

$$n! = n \times (n-1)! \tag{6}$$

Initially, Gamma faced challenges in implementing the recursive function. The joy lay not only in arriving at the correct solution but also in understanding the underlying principles of recursion and the elegance of the solution itself. Each successful implementation brought a rush of satisfaction, reinforcing his passion for coding.

Creativity and Expression

Beyond problem-solving, coding offered Gamma a unique form of self-expression. Each program he wrote became a canvas on which he painted his ideas. The ability to create software that could interact with users, manipulate data, and automate tasks was exhilarating. He found joy in transforming abstract concepts into functional applications.

For example, Gamma developed a simple text-based game that allowed users to navigate through a maze. The logic required to design the game mechanics, coupled with the creativity involved in crafting an engaging user experience, highlighted the dual nature of programming as both a science and an art.

$$Score = Points\ Earned - Time\ Taken \tag{7}$$

This equation, representing the scoring system in his game, exemplifies how coding can quantify experiences and create interactive narratives. The joy of coding, therefore, lies in its ability to blend logic with creativity, resulting in solutions that are both functional and imaginative.

Mentorship and Community

As Gamma's skills grew, so did his appreciation for the programming community. He found mentors who nurtured his passion, providing guidance and encouragement. The collaborative spirit within the programming community further fueled his enthusiasm. Engaging with peers, sharing ideas, and tackling challenges together created a sense of belonging that enriched his journey.

The joy of coding was amplified by the realization that he was part of a larger movement—one that sought to innovate and push the boundaries of technology. This realization was pivotal in shaping Gamma's identity as a programmer, as he began to understand the impact of his work on the world around him.

Conclusion

In summary, the discovery of coding for Erich Gamma was a transformative experience. It was a journey filled with excitement, creativity, and growth. The joy derived from problem-solving, the thrill of creating functional applications, and the sense of community all contributed to his development as a programmer. This foundational joy would propel him forward, leading to groundbreaking contributions in the field of software development, including the revolutionary concept of design patterns.

Thus, the untold story of Erich Gamma's early experiences in coding serves as a testament to the power of discovery and the profound impact of finding joy in one's work. As he embarked on this path, he not only shaped his own destiny but also laid the groundwork for innovations that would change the software industry forever.

Nurturing the passion for problem-solving

The journey of Erich Gamma into the realm of programming was not merely a chance encounter with technology; it was a profound exploration of the art of problem-solving. This innate curiosity and desire to tackle complex challenges became the cornerstone of his identity as a programmer.

The Essence of Problem-Solving

At its core, problem-solving in programming involves identifying a challenge, analyzing potential solutions, and implementing the most effective approach. This process can be broken down into several key stages:

1. **Problem Identification:** Recognizing that a problem exists is the first step. This often involves understanding user needs, system limitations, or unexpected behavior in software.

2. **Analysis:** Once a problem is identified, the next step is to analyze it. This includes gathering data, understanding the context, and breaking down the problem into smaller, manageable components.

3. **Solution Development:** After thorough analysis, programmers brainstorm potential solutions. This stage may involve creative thinking and leveraging existing knowledge and tools.

4. **Implementation:** The chosen solution is then implemented through coding. This is where theoretical knowledge meets practical application.

5. **Testing and Evaluation:** Finally, the solution is tested to ensure it effectively resolves the problem. Feedback is gathered, and adjustments are made as necessary.

Theoretical Foundations

In nurturing a passion for problem-solving, several theoretical frameworks can be applied. One such framework is the *Polya's Four Steps of Problem Solving*, which includes:

1. **Understanding the Problem:** This involves clarifying what is being asked and identifying the unknowns.

2. **Devising a Plan:** Formulating a strategy to tackle the problem, which may involve drawing diagrams or writing pseudocode.

3. **Carrying Out the Plan:** Implementing the plan through coding and debugging.

4. **Looking Back:** Reflecting on the solution and considering alternative approaches or improvements.

This structured approach not only aids in solving programming challenges but also fosters a mindset geared toward continuous learning and adaptation.

Real-World Examples

Erich Gamma's early exposure to problem-solving can be illustrated through his interactions with various programming languages and projects. For instance, during his formative years, Gamma encountered the challenge of developing efficient algorithms for data processing.

One notable problem he faced involved optimizing a sorting algorithm. Initially, he implemented a straightforward bubble sort algorithm, which had a time complexity of $O(n^2)$:

$$\text{Bubble Sort: } T(n) = n(n-1)/2 \tag{8}$$

However, as he delved deeper into the intricacies of algorithm design, he recognized the need for efficiency, especially when handling larger datasets. This realization led him to explore more advanced algorithms, such as quicksort, which operates with an average time complexity of $O(n \log n)$:

$$\text{Quicksort: } T(n) = n \log n \tag{9}$$

By experimenting with different approaches and analyzing their performance, Gamma not only solved the immediate problem but also developed a robust understanding of algorithmic efficiency.

The Role of Mentorship and Collaboration

Throughout his journey, Gamma was fortunate to have mentors who recognized and nurtured his passion for problem-solving. These mentors encouraged him to tackle increasingly complex challenges, fostering an environment where creativity and critical thinking flourished. Collaborative projects with peers also played a significant role in shaping his problem-solving abilities.

For example, during group projects at Zurich University, Gamma and his colleagues would often engage in brainstorming sessions, where they would collectively dissect problems and propose innovative solutions. This collaborative spirit not only enriched his learning experience but also reinforced the idea that problem-solving is often best approached through diverse perspectives.

Conclusion

Nurturing a passion for problem-solving is an essential aspect of becoming a successful programmer. For Erich Gamma, this passion was cultivated through structured methodologies, real-world challenges, and the influence of mentors and peers. As he continued to evolve in his career, this foundational skill would enable him to contribute significantly to the field of software development, particularly through his groundbreaking work on design patterns. The journey of problem-solving is not just about finding solutions; it is about embracing the complexities of challenges and continuously striving for excellence.

The mentors who shaped Gamma's path

Throughout his formative years, Erich Gamma was fortunate to encounter a series of mentors who profoundly influenced his journey into the world of programming and software design. These individuals not only imparted technical knowledge but also instilled in him the values of creativity, critical thinking, and perseverance. In this section, we will explore the significant figures who played pivotal roles in shaping Gamma's path.

Early Influencers in Zurich

In the serene surroundings of Zurich, Gamma's early mentors emerged from both academic and personal spheres. One of the first influential figures was his high school mathematics teacher, Herr Müller. Known for his unconventional teaching methods, Herr Müller encouraged students to approach problems from multiple angles. He often posed complex mathematical puzzles that required not just rote memorization but also innovative thinking. This pedagogical style resonated with Gamma, who found joy in unraveling intricate problems and developing unique solutions.

Another crucial mentor during Gamma's teenage years was his neighbor, an engineer named Frau Schneider. She worked on software development projects and often invited Gamma to observe her work. It was during these informal sessions that Gamma first encountered programming languages. Frau Schneider's enthusiasm for technology and her willingness to share her knowledge ignited a spark in Gamma. She introduced him to the fundamentals of coding, teaching him how to write simple programs in BASIC. This early exposure laid the groundwork for Gamma's burgeoning interest in software development.

University Mentorship

Upon entering Zurich University, Gamma encountered a new set of mentors who would further refine his programming skills and philosophical outlook on software design. One of the most notable figures was Professor Hans Gruber, a leading expert in computer science and a pioneer of object-oriented programming (OOP). Under Professor Gruber's guidance, Gamma delved deeper into the principles of OOP, learning about encapsulation, inheritance, and polymorphism. Gruber's lectures were not just theoretical; they were filled with real-world applications and case studies that demonstrated the power of OOP in solving complex software problems.

Professor Gruber's mentorship extended beyond the classroom. He encouraged Gamma to participate in research projects, fostering a collaborative environment where students could experiment with new ideas. One such project involved developing a software prototype for a local business, which allowed Gamma to apply his theoretical knowledge in a practical setting. This experience not only honed his technical skills but also taught him the importance of teamwork and communication in software development.

Influence of Industry Leaders

As Gamma progressed through his academic career, he had the opportunity to interact with industry leaders who were at the forefront of software innovation. One such figure was Dr. Klaus Jansen, a renowned software architect and one of the early adopters of design patterns in software engineering. Dr. Jansen conducted workshops and seminars at the university, where he shared his insights on the significance of design patterns in creating robust software architectures.

During one of these workshops, Gamma was introduced to the concept of design patterns as reusable solutions to common software design problems. Dr. Jansen's ability to articulate complex ideas in an accessible manner inspired Gamma to explore this field further. He encouraged Gamma to think critically about software design and to consider how design patterns could streamline development processes and improve code maintainability.

The Gang of Four

The culmination of Gamma's mentorship experience came when he collaborated with fellow students and industry leaders who would later become known as the "Gang of Four." This group, which included Richard Helm, Ralph Johnson, and John Vlissides, was instrumental in formalizing the concept of design patterns in software engineering. Their diverse backgrounds and expertise created a rich environment for brainstorming and innovation.

Under the guidance of these mentors, Gamma contributed to the seminal book *Design Patterns: Elements of Reusable Object-Oriented Software*, which would go on to revolutionize software development practices. The collaborative spirit fostered by the Gang of Four allowed Gamma to learn from his peers while also sharing his unique insights. Together, they tackled the initial skepticism surrounding design patterns, conducting extensive research and analysis to validate their concepts.

Conclusion

The mentors who shaped Erich Gamma's path were not merely teachers; they were catalysts for his growth as a programmer and innovator. From the early influences in Zurich to the collaborative efforts with the Gang of Four, each mentor played a vital role in nurturing Gamma's talents and guiding him toward his eventual contributions to the field of software engineering. Their collective wisdom and encouragement instilled in him a lifelong passion for problem-solving and a commitment to excellence in software design, laying the foundation for his legacy as a pioneer in the world of design patterns.

$$\text{Mentorship Impact} = \sum_{i=1}^{n} \text{Influence}_i \tag{10}$$

Where Influence_i represents the impact of each mentor on Gamma's development, and n is the total number of mentors encountered throughout his journey.

University Years and Beyond

Entrance into Zurich University

Majoring in computer science

Erich Gamma's journey through academia began with his enrollment at Zurich University, where he chose to major in computer science. This decision was pivotal, not only for his career but also for the evolution of software engineering as a discipline. During the late 1970s and early 1980s, the field of computer science was rapidly evolving, and Gamma found himself at the forefront of this transformation.

Foundations of Computer Science

The curriculum at Zurich University was rigorous, emphasizing both theoretical foundations and practical applications. Students were introduced to key concepts such as algorithms, data structures, and computational theory. One of the fundamental theories that Gamma encountered was the **Big O notation**, which provides a high-level understanding of algorithm efficiency.

$$O(n) = \text{Linear Time Complexity} \tag{11}$$

This notation allowed Gamma to analyze the performance of algorithms, a skill that would prove invaluable in his future work on design patterns. For instance, understanding the efficiency of searching algorithms like binary search, which operates in $O(\log n)$ time, versus linear search, which operates in $O(n)$ time, was crucial in developing efficient software solutions.

Practical Programming Experience

In addition to theoretical knowledge, Gamma's coursework included extensive programming assignments that required him to implement various algorithms and data structures. He became proficient in languages such as C and Pascal, which were popular at the time.

One notable project involved creating a simple text editor, where Gamma applied his understanding of linked lists to manage text buffers. The challenge of handling dynamic memory allocation and ensuring efficient performance sparked his interest in software architecture.

Emergence of Object-Oriented Programming

During his time at university, Gamma was introduced to the emerging paradigm of **object-oriented programming** (OOP). This approach revolutionized software development by allowing programmers to model real-world entities through objects, encapsulating data and behavior. Concepts such as inheritance, polymorphism, and encapsulation became central to his understanding of software design.

Gamma's exposure to OOP coincided with the development of programming languages that supported this paradigm, such as Smalltalk. The ability to create reusable code through class hierarchies and interfaces fascinated him and laid the groundwork for his future contributions to design patterns.

Collaborative Projects and Teamwork

Collaboration was a key component of Gamma's education. He participated in group projects that simulated real-world software development environments. These experiences taught him the importance of teamwork, communication, and project management.

One memorable project involved developing a simulation of a banking system, where each team member was responsible for a specific module, such as account management or transaction processing. This experience highlighted the significance of modular design and the need for clear interfaces between components, concepts that would later be encapsulated in design patterns.

Influential Mentors and Faculty

Gamma was fortunate to have mentors who recognized his potential and encouraged his interest in computer science. Professors at Zurich University were not only knowledgeable but also passionate about their fields, inspiring students to think critically and creatively.

One such mentor, Professor Hanspeter Mössenböck, introduced Gamma to the principles of software engineering and the importance of design methodologies. Under his guidance, Gamma learned about the need for systematic approaches to software development, which would later influence his work on the **Gang of Four** design patterns.

Conclusion: A Launchpad for Innovation

Majoring in computer science at Zurich University provided Erich Gamma with a solid foundation in both theoretical principles and practical programming skills. The challenges he faced and the knowledge he gained during these formative years prepared him for a career that would significantly impact the software development landscape. As he delved deeper into object-oriented programming and software design, the stage was set for Gamma to emerge as a leading figure in the field, ultimately contributing to the creation of design patterns that would shape the future of programming.

In summary, Gamma's university experience was not merely an academic pursuit; it was a transformative journey that ignited his passion for coding and problem-solving, propelling him toward a legacy of innovation in software engineering.

Formative experiences at Zurich University

Erich Gamma's journey at Zurich University was a pivotal chapter in his evolution as a programmer and thinker. Enrolling in the computer science program, he found himself immersed in a rich academic environment that not only fostered technical skills but also encouraged critical thinking and innovation. The university's emphasis on a strong theoretical foundation in computer science laid the groundwork for Gamma's future contributions to the field.

One of the formative experiences during his university years was the exposure to various programming paradigms. Gamma encountered the principles of structured programming, which emphasized a clear flow of control and the use of functions to manage complexity. This was a stark contrast to the more chaotic approaches that were prevalent in earlier programming practices. The structured programming paradigm, as articulated by Dijkstra [?], emphasized the importance of logical reasoning in programming, leading to more reliable and maintainable code.

$$\text{Structured Program} = \text{Sequence} + \text{Selection} + \text{Iteration} \tag{12}$$

As Gamma delved deeper into the coursework, he was introduced to the concepts of data abstraction and modular programming. The idea of encapsulating data and behavior within modules resonated with him, as it mirrored the way complex systems could be understood and managed. This exposure was instrumental in shaping his understanding of object-oriented programming (OOP), which he would later champion.

In addition to the theoretical underpinnings, practical experiences at Zurich University played a significant role in Gamma's development. He participated in collaborative projects that simulated real-world software development scenarios. These projects often involved solving complex problems, such as optimizing algorithms for performance or designing user interfaces that were both functional and aesthetically pleasing. One notable project involved developing a simple text editor, where Gamma and his peers had to navigate the challenges of user input handling and file management, which are critical components of software applications.

Through these hands-on experiences, Gamma learned the importance of iterative development and user feedback. He became aware of the necessity to adapt and refine software based on user interactions, a principle that would later influence his work on design patterns. The iterative process is encapsulated in the Agile Manifesto [?], which emphasizes the value of responding to change over following a fixed plan.

Moreover, Gamma was fortunate to be mentored by professors who were pioneers in the field of computer science. Their guidance not only inspired him but also instilled a sense of curiosity and a desire to push the boundaries of what was possible in programming. The discussions in the classroom often extended beyond the syllabus, exploring philosophical questions about the nature of computation and the ethical implications of technology.

The university's collaborative culture also fostered relationships with fellow students who would become lifelong friends and colleagues. These connections proved invaluable as they shared ideas, challenged each other's thinking, and collaborated on projects that would later influence their careers. The camaraderie among students created an environment ripe for innovation, where brainstorming sessions could lead to breakthroughs in understanding complex programming concepts.

In summary, Erich Gamma's formative experiences at Zurich University were marked by a blend of rigorous academic training, practical problem-solving, and collaborative learning. The exposure to structured programming, data abstraction, and iterative development not only equipped him with essential skills but also ignited a passion for software design that would define his career. These experiences laid the foundation for his future work in object-oriented programming and the creation of design patterns, which would ultimately transform the software industry.

Emergence of Gamma as a programming prodigy

As Erich Gamma embarked on his academic journey at Zurich University, the stage was set for a remarkable transformation. With a burgeoning interest in computer science, Gamma quickly distinguished himself as a student with exceptional aptitude and an insatiable curiosity for programming. This section will delve into the factors that contributed to his emergence as a programming prodigy, highlighting key experiences, challenges, and theoretical foundations that shaped his early career.

Academic Excellence and Innovation

Gamma's academic prowess was evident from the outset. He approached his studies with a unique blend of creativity and analytical thinking, which allowed him to grasp complex concepts with remarkable ease. His coursework in computer science included a variety of subjects, from algorithms to software engineering principles. One particularly influential course was on data structures, where he learned to manipulate and optimize data efficiently. This foundational knowledge would later play a crucial role in his development of design patterns.

The concept of a *data structure* can be mathematically defined as a way of organizing and storing data so that it can be accessed and modified efficiently. For instance, consider the following equation representing the time complexity of accessing an element in an array:

$$T(n) = O(1)$$

This equation illustrates that accessing an element in an array is a constant time operation, which is a fundamental principle that Gamma would later apply in his design patterns.

Collaborative Projects and Early Contributions

During his university years, Gamma actively engaged in collaborative projects that showcased his programming skills. He participated in hackathons and coding competitions, where he not only honed his technical abilities but also learned the importance of teamwork and communication in software development. One notable project involved developing a simple text editor, which introduced him to the intricacies of user interface design and the significance of user experience.

In this project, Gamma and his team faced several challenges, including optimizing the performance of the editor and ensuring it could handle multiple file formats. They implemented various algorithms to manage memory efficiently, demonstrating an early understanding of software optimization. This experience laid the groundwork for his later work in design patterns, where efficiency and usability are paramount.

Mentorship and Influential Figures

Gamma's growth as a programmer was significantly influenced by mentors who recognized his potential. One such figure was Professor Müller, a renowned expert in object-oriented programming. Under his guidance, Gamma was introduced to the principles of object-oriented design, which would become a cornerstone of his future contributions.

Theoretical foundations of object-oriented programming emphasize the use of *classes* and *objects* to encapsulate data and behavior. The following equation represents the relationship between a class and its objects:

$$O = C \times n$$

Where O is the total number of objects, C is the number of classes, and n is the number of instances per class. This equation illustrates the scalability of object-oriented design, a principle that Gamma would later leverage in his work on design patterns.

Recognition and Early Achievements

As Gamma progressed through his studies, his innovative ideas and contributions began to gain recognition. He published his first research paper on efficient sorting algorithms, which showcased his ability to tackle complex problems with elegant solutions. This paper not only earned him accolades from his peers but also established him as a thought leader in the emerging field of software engineering.

Furthermore, Gamma's participation in international conferences allowed him to network with industry leaders and gain insights into the latest trends and technologies. These experiences further fueled his passion for programming and solidified his commitment to advancing the field.

Conclusion: The Prodigy Emerges

By the time Gamma graduated from Zurich University, he had already established himself as a programming prodigy. His combination of academic excellence, collaborative spirit, and innovative thinking set the stage for his future endeavors in software development. The experiences he gained during these formative years not only shaped his technical skills but also instilled in him a deep appreciation for the art of programming.

As we look back on this pivotal period in Gamma's life, it becomes clear that his emergence as a programming prodigy was not merely a result of talent, but also a reflection of the nurturing environment that fostered his growth. This foundation would eventually lead him to become one of the most influential figures in software engineering, paving the way for the development of design patterns that continue to shape the industry today.

Joining the Object-Oriented Programming Movement

Introduction to object-oriented concepts

Object-oriented programming (OOP) is a programming paradigm that utilizes the concept of "objects," which can contain data in the form of fields (often known as attributes or properties) and code in the form of procedures (often known as methods). OOP is built around several key concepts that facilitate code organization, reuse, and scalability. This section delves into the fundamental principles of OOP, its theoretical foundations, and practical implications.

Key Principles of Object-Oriented Programming

The primary principles of OOP are encapsulation, inheritance, polymorphism, and abstraction. Each principle plays a crucial role in the design and implementation of robust software systems.

- **Encapsulation** is the bundling of data with the methods that operate on that data. This principle restricts direct access to some of an object's components, which can prevent the accidental modification of data. Encapsulation is achieved through access modifiers such as private, public, and protected.

- **Inheritance** allows a new class, known as a subclass or derived class, to inherit properties and methods from an existing class, known as a superclass or base class. This promotes code reuse and establishes a hierarchical relationship between classes. For example, if we have a class `Animal`, a subclass `Dog` can inherit characteristics from `Animal`.

- **Polymorphism** is the ability for different classes to be treated as instances of the same class through a common interface. It allows methods to do different things based on the object it is acting upon. For instance, both Dog and Cat can implement a method makeSound(), but each will produce a different output.

+ **Abstraction** simplifies complex reality by modeling classes based on the essential properties and behaviors an object should have. This means that the implementation details are hidden while exposing only the necessary parts of the object. Abstract classes and interfaces are common ways to achieve abstraction in OOP.

Theoretical Foundations of OOP

The theoretical underpinnings of OOP can be traced back to the need for more modular and maintainable code. Early programming paradigms, such as procedural programming, often led to monolithic code structures that were difficult to manage. OOP addresses these challenges by promoting a more structured approach.

The concept of an *object* can be mathematically represented as a pair (D, M) where D is a set of data (attributes) and M is a set of methods (functions) that operate on that data. This can be formally expressed as:

$$O = (D, M)$$

Where:

+ $D = \{d_1, d_2, \ldots, d_n\}$ represents the attributes of the object.

+ $M = \{m_1, m_2, \ldots, m_k\}$ represents the methods of the object.

This encapsulation of data and behavior allows for the creation of self-contained modules, which can be easily manipulated and reused across various parts of a software application.

Common Problems Addressed by OOP

OOP addresses several common problems faced in software development:

+ **Code Duplication:** OOP promotes code reuse through inheritance and polymorphism, significantly reducing redundancy. For example, a base class Vehicle can encapsulate common properties like speed and methods like move(), which can be inherited by subclasses such as Car and Bike.

- **Complexity Management:** By breaking down complex systems into smaller, manageable objects, OOP allows developers to focus on individual components without losing sight of the overall system architecture. This modular approach simplifies the debugging and maintenance processes.

- **Scalability:** OOP systems can be easily extended by adding new classes without modifying existing code. This is particularly beneficial in large software projects where requirements frequently change.

- **Data Security:** Through encapsulation, OOP restricts access to an object's internal state, allowing developers to control how the data is accessed and modified. This enhances data integrity and security within applications.

Examples of Object-Oriented Concepts

To illustrate the concepts discussed, consider the following example in a hypothetical programming language:

```
class Animal {
    protected String\index{String} name\index{name};

    public Animal(String name) {
        this.name = name;
    }

    public void makeSound() {
        System.out.println("Some sound");
    }
}

class Dog extends Animal {
    public Dog(String name) {
        super(name);
    }

    @Override
    public void makeSound() {
        System.out.println(name + `` says Woof!");
    }
}
```

```
class Cat extends Animal {
    public Cat(String name) {
        super(name);
    }

    @Override
    public void makeSound() {
        System.out.println(name + `` says Meow!");
    }
}

public class Main {
    public static void main(String[] args) {
        Animal myDog = new Dog("Buddy");
        Animal myCat = new Cat("Whiskers");

        myDog.makeSound(); // Outputs: Buddy says Woof!
        myCat.makeSound(); // Outputs: Whiskers says Meow!
    }
}
```

In this example, we define a base class Animal with a method makeSound(). The subclasses Dog and Cat inherit from Animal and provide their specific implementations of makeSound(). This demonstrates inheritance and polymorphism in action.

Conclusion

The introduction of object-oriented concepts has revolutionized the way software is developed. By leveraging encapsulation, inheritance, polymorphism, and abstraction, programmers can create more organized, maintainable, and scalable code. Understanding these principles is essential for any aspiring software developer and lays the groundwork for advanced programming techniques and methodologies.

Gamma's role in advancing object-oriented programming

Erich Gamma's contributions to the field of object-oriented programming (OOP) are not merely footnotes in the history of software development; they represent pivotal moments that have shaped the trajectory of programming paradigms. As a member of the influential "Gang of Four," Gamma played a crucial role in popularizing and formalizing concepts that would become foundational to OOP.

Understanding Object-Oriented Programming

At its core, OOP is a programming paradigm that utilizes "objects" to represent data and methods. Objects encapsulate both state (attributes) and behavior (methods), promoting modularity and reusability. Key principles of OOP include:

+ **Encapsulation:** Bundling data and methods that operate on the data within one unit (the object).

+ **Inheritance:** A mechanism whereby a new class can inherit properties and behavior from an existing class.

+ **Polymorphism:** The ability to present the same interface for different underlying data types.

These principles enable developers to create more maintainable and scalable code. However, as programming grew more complex, the need for design patterns—standardized solutions to common problems—became increasingly apparent.

Gamma's Contributions to OOP

Gamma's role in advancing OOP can be dissected into several key contributions:

1. The Gang of Four Book   In 1994, Gamma, along with Richard Helm, Ralph Johnson, and John Vlissides, published the seminal book titled *Design Patterns: Elements of Reusable Object-Oriented Software*. This work not only cataloged 23 design patterns but also provided a common vocabulary for discussing OOP concepts. The patterns were categorized into three types:

+ **Creational Patterns:** Patterns that deal with object creation mechanisms, aiming to create objects in a manner suitable to the situation. Examples include the *Factory Method* and *Singleton*.

+ **Structural Patterns:** Patterns that deal with object composition, helping to ensure that if one part of a system changes, the entire system does not need to change. Examples include the *Adapter* and *Decorator*.

+ **Behavioral Patterns:** Patterns that focus on communication between objects. Examples include the *Observer* and *Strategy*.

The book's influence is profound, as it shifted the focus from mere coding to design, encouraging developers to think about the architecture of their applications.

2. **Promoting Best Practices**   Gamma's advocacy for best practices in OOP extended beyond the book. He actively participated in discussions at conferences and workshops, helping to disseminate the principles of OOP and design patterns. His presentations often included practical examples that demonstrated how to implement these patterns effectively, bridging the gap between theory and practice.

3. **Object Technology and Frameworks**   Gamma's work did not stop at design patterns; he also contributed to the development of object-oriented frameworks. His involvement in the development of the *Eclipse* platform exemplifies this. Eclipse, an open-source IDE, is built on object-oriented principles and showcases the power of design patterns in creating extensible software. The use of design patterns in Eclipse not only facilitated the development of plugins but also established a model for future IDEs.

Challenges and Solutions in OOP

Despite the advantages of OOP, it is not without challenges. One of the primary issues is the complexity that arises from excessive abstraction and over-engineering. Gamma recognized this problem and emphasized the importance of simplicity in design. He advocated for the principle of *YAGNI* (You Aren't Gonna Need It), which encourages developers to avoid adding functionality until it is necessary.

Additionally, the misuse of design patterns can lead to what is known as *design pattern overkill*, where developers apply patterns inappropriately, complicating rather than simplifying the code. Gamma's teachings often focused on understanding when and how to apply patterns effectively, ensuring that they serve their intended purpose without introducing unnecessary complexity.

Real-World Examples

To illustrate Gamma's impact, consider the *Observer Pattern*. This pattern is widely used in event-driven systems, such as graphical user interfaces (GUIs). For instance, in a weather application, multiple displays (observers) can subscribe to a weather data source (subject). When the weather data changes, all subscribed displays are automatically updated, showcasing the power of decoupling components.

Another example is the *Strategy Pattern*, which allows a family of algorithms to be defined and encapsulated so that they can be interchanged. This pattern is commonly used in sorting algorithms, where different strategies (like quicksort or mergesort) can be applied without altering the core functionality of the application.

Conclusion

Erich Gamma's role in advancing object-oriented programming is characterized by his commitment to promoting best practices, formalizing design patterns, and addressing the challenges inherent in OOP. His contributions have left an indelible mark on the software development landscape, inspiring generations of programmers to embrace the principles of OOP and design patterns in their work. As the field of programming continues to evolve, Gamma's insights remain relevant, guiding developers toward creating robust, maintainable, and scalable software solutions.

Collaborations with industry leaders

Erich Gamma's journey into the realm of programming was not one he undertook alone. Throughout his career, he forged significant collaborations with industry leaders that not only shaped his own understanding of software development but also influenced the trajectory of programming as a discipline. These partnerships were pivotal in the evolution of object-oriented programming (OOP) and the eventual emergence of design patterns.

The Role of Collaboration in Software Development

Collaboration in software engineering is essential, as it allows for the pooling of diverse expertise and perspectives. As noted by [?], "collaboration is the lifeblood of software development, fostering innovation and ensuring the robustness of solutions." This principle was particularly true for Gamma, who thrived in environments where ideas could be exchanged freely.

Key Collaborators

One of Gamma's most notable collaborations was with his peers at the University of Zurich, where he worked alongside influential figures such as Richard Helm, Ralph Johnson, and John Vlissides. This group, later known as the "Gang of Four," laid the groundwork for the seminal book *Design Patterns: Elements of Reusable Object-Oriented Software*, published in 1994. Their collective expertise in various programming paradigms enabled them to identify common problems in software design and articulate solutions that would become foundational to modern software engineering.

The Gang of Four and Their Contributions

The Gang of Four approached the concept of design patterns with a structured methodology, which can be summarized in the following key stages:

- **Identification of Patterns:** The team conducted extensive research to identify recurring design issues in software projects. They analyzed existing systems to distill commonalities and categorize them into patterns.

- **Documentation and Analysis:** Each pattern was meticulously documented, detailing its applicability, structure, and consequences. This structured documentation allowed practitioners to understand not just the "how," but also the "why" behind each pattern.

- **Validation through Real-world Examples:** The patterns were validated against real-world software projects. For instance, the Singleton pattern was illustrated through its use in managing a shared resource, demonstrating its effectiveness in controlling access to a single instance of a class.

The collaboration culminated in the establishment of 23 design patterns that addressed various aspects of software design, including Creational, Structural, and Behavioral patterns. Each category serves a distinct purpose:

$$\text{Total Patterns} = \text{Creational} + \text{Structural} + \text{Behavioral} \qquad (13)$$

where:

- **Creational Patterns** focus on object creation mechanisms, aiming to create objects in a manner suitable to the situation.

- **Structural Patterns** deal with object composition, ensuring that if one part of a system changes, the entire system does not need to do the same.

- **Behavioral Patterns** are concerned with algorithms and the assignment of responsibilities between objects.

Real-world Impact of Collaborations

The impact of Gamma's collaborations is evident in the widespread adoption of design patterns across the software industry. For instance, the Observer pattern has been instrumental in developing event-driven systems, such as those used in graphical user interfaces (GUIs). The implementation of this pattern allows for a clean separation between the subject and observers, facilitating more manageable and scalable code.

Another significant outcome of these collaborations was the establishment of the concept of "design pattern languages." This concept, as discussed by [?], emphasizes the importance of context in software design. Gamma and his colleagues expanded this idea to software engineering, advocating for patterns that could be adapted to specific scenarios, thus enhancing flexibility and reusability.

Challenges Faced in Collaboration

Despite the success of these collaborations, challenges were prevalent. Differing opinions on design philosophies often led to heated debates. For example, while some members of the Gang of Four favored strict adherence to OOP principles, others advocated for a more pragmatic approach that allowed for procedural programming techniques. Such disagreements necessitated a careful balancing act, ensuring that all voices were heard while maintaining a unified vision.

Moreover, the collaborative process required navigating the complexities of authorship and credit. The recognition of contributions became a contentious issue, particularly when it came to the publication of their work. Gamma and his colleagues had to establish clear guidelines to ensure that each member's contributions were acknowledged appropriately.

Conclusion

In summary, Erich Gamma's collaborations with industry leaders were instrumental in shaping both his career and the field of software engineering. The synergy created within the Gang of Four not only led to the development of design patterns but also fostered a culture of knowledge sharing that continues to influence programmers today. Through these collaborative efforts, Gamma and his peers have left an indelible mark on the software development landscape, proving that great ideas often emerge from the collective genius of passionate individuals working together.

The Birth of Design Patterns

Design Patterns: A breakthrough in software architecture

Understanding the significance

The concept of design patterns revolutionized software engineering, offering a systematic approach to solving common problems in software design. At its core, a design pattern is a reusable solution to a recurring design problem within a given context. This section delves into the significance of design patterns, exploring their theoretical foundations, practical applications, and the profound impact they have had on software development.

Theoretical Foundations

Design patterns are rooted in the principles of object-oriented design, which emphasize the importance of modularity, encapsulation, and abstraction. The seminal work by Gamma et al. in "Design Patterns: Elements of Reusable Object-Oriented Software" introduced a catalog of 23 design patterns that encapsulate best practices in software design. Each pattern provides a blueprint for addressing specific challenges, thereby promoting code reusability and maintainability.

One of the key theoretical underpinnings of design patterns is the **SOLID** principles, which serve as guidelines for creating robust and flexible software architectures. The SOLID principles are:

- **Single Responsibility Principle (SRP):** A class should have only one reason to change, meaning it should have only one job or responsibility.

+ **Open/Closed Principle (OCP):** Software entities should be open for extension but closed for modification, allowing for new functionality without altering existing code.

+ **Liskov Substitution Principle (LSP):** Objects of a superclass should be replaceable with objects of a subclass without affecting the correctness of the program.

+ **Interface Segregation Principle (ISP):** Clients should not be forced to depend on interfaces they do not use, promoting smaller, more specific interfaces.

+ **Dependency Inversion Principle (DIP):** High-level modules should not depend on low-level modules; both should depend on abstractions.

These principles align closely with the intent of design patterns, providing a theoretical framework that enhances the understanding and application of design solutions.

Practical Applications

The practical significance of design patterns is evident in their ability to address common problems encountered during software development. For instance, consider the **Singleton** pattern, which ensures that a class has only one instance and provides a global point of access to it. This is particularly useful in scenarios such as logging, where a single logging instance is required to maintain a consistent log state.

The implementation of the Singleton pattern can be illustrated as follows:

```
class Singleton {
private:
    static Singleton* instance;

    // Private constructor to prevent instantiation
    Singleton() {}

public:
    static Singleton* getInstance() {
        if (!instance) {
            instance = new Singleton();
```

```
        }
        return\index{return} instance\index{instance};
    }
};
```

In this example, the Singleton pattern encapsulates the instantiation logic, ensuring that only one instance of the class exists throughout the application. This not only simplifies the code but also enhances maintainability by centralizing the instance management.

Another critical design pattern is the **Observer** pattern, which establishes a one-to-many dependency between objects, allowing multiple observers to be notified of changes in the subject's state. This pattern is widely used in event-driven programming, such as in graphical user interfaces (GUIs) and real-time data processing systems.

An example of the Observer pattern can be represented as follows:

```
class Subject {
private:
    std::list<Observer*> observers;

public:
    void attach(Observer* observer) {
        observers.push_back(observer);
    }

    void notify() {
        for (Observer* observer : observers) {
            observer->update();
        }
    }
};
```

In this scenario, the Subject maintains a list of observers and notifies them of any state changes, promoting loose coupling between the components.

Impact on Software Development

The introduction of design patterns has had a transformative impact on the software development industry. By providing a shared vocabulary and common solutions, design patterns facilitate communication among developers, making it easier to discuss design challenges and solutions.

Moreover, the adoption of design patterns enhances code quality and reduces technical debt. By adhering to established patterns, developers can create code that is easier to understand, test, and maintain. This leads to increased productivity and reduced time spent on debugging and refactoring.

The significance of design patterns is also evident in their role in fostering collaboration and knowledge sharing within development teams. Patterns serve as a reference point for best practices, enabling developers to build upon each other's work and innovate more effectively.

Conclusion

In summary, the significance of design patterns extends far beyond mere coding techniques; they represent a paradigm shift in how software is designed and developed. By encapsulating proven solutions to common problems, design patterns empower developers to create robust, maintainable, and scalable software systems. As the software industry continues to evolve, the principles and practices encapsulated in design patterns will remain foundational to the craft of programming, ensuring their relevance for generations to come.

Initial challenges and skepticism

The introduction of design patterns into the software engineering landscape was not without its hurdles. As Erich Gamma and his colleagues embarked on their journey to document these patterns, they faced significant initial challenges and skepticism from both academia and industry practitioners. This section delves into the various obstacles they encountered, the prevailing doubts about the utility of design patterns, and the theoretical underpinnings that fueled the discourse surrounding their adoption.

Resistance to Change

One of the foremost challenges was the inherent resistance to change within the software development community. Many programmers were accustomed to their established practices and methodologies, often viewing design patterns as unnecessary complications. The skepticism was rooted in a broader reluctance to adopt new paradigms that deviated from procedural programming, which had dominated the field for decades.

"If it ain't broke, don't fix it."

This adage encapsulated the mindset of many developers who were skeptical about the need for design patterns. They questioned whether the investment in learning and implementing these patterns would yield tangible benefits in their day-to-day programming tasks.

Defining Patterns: A Conceptual Challenge

Another significant challenge was the conceptual difficulty in defining what constituted a design pattern. Christopher Alexander's original work in architecture provided a foundational framework, but translating these ideas into software engineering was complex. The authors had to grapple with questions such as:

+ What differentiates a design pattern from a mere coding trick?

+ How do we ensure that patterns are general enough to be applicable in various contexts?

+ What criteria should be used to classify and document these patterns effectively?

To address these questions, Gamma and his colleagues proposed a structure for documenting design patterns, which included the following elements:

+ **Name:** A descriptive title for the pattern.

+ **Problem:** The specific issue the pattern addresses.

+ **Solution:** The proposed solution encapsulated in the pattern.

+ **Consequences:** The potential trade-offs and impacts of using the pattern.

This structured approach was pivotal in clarifying the purpose and utility of design patterns, but it took time for the community to embrace this new framework.

Skepticism from Academia

In academia, skepticism was often rooted in a desire for rigor and empirical validation. Many scholars questioned the lack of formal methodologies for evaluating the effectiveness of design patterns. They argued that without empirical studies demonstrating the benefits of using design patterns, their adoption could not be justified.

In response to these critiques, Gamma and his colleagues began to gather case studies and examples from the industry to illustrate the real-world applications of design patterns. They highlighted instances where design patterns had led to improved code maintainability, increased collaboration among developers, and enhanced scalability in software projects.

$$\text{Maintainability} \propto \frac{1}{\text{Complexity}} \tag{14}$$

This equation succinctly encapsulates the relationship between maintainability and complexity, suggesting that by employing design patterns, developers could reduce complexity in their codebases, thereby enhancing maintainability.

The Role of Communication

Effective communication played a crucial role in overcoming skepticism. Gamma and his team engaged in discussions and presentations at conferences, workshops, and meetups to share their findings and experiences with design patterns. They utilized storytelling techniques to convey the value of patterns, often framing them as tools that could empower developers to tackle complex problems with confidence.

> "Design patterns are not just solutions; they are a common language for developers."

This perspective helped to foster a sense of community around design patterns, allowing developers to see them not merely as abstract concepts but as practical tools that could enhance their craft.

Conclusion

Despite the initial challenges and skepticism surrounding design patterns, Erich Gamma and his colleagues persevered, laying the groundwork for a paradigm shift in software development. Their efforts to define, document, and promote design patterns ultimately led to their widespread acceptance and integration into the software engineering lexicon. The journey from skepticism to acceptance was not instantaneous, but it was marked by a commitment to education, communication, and collaboration that would forever change the landscape of software design.

Collaborative efforts with the "Gang of Four"

The term "Gang of Four" (GoF) refers to the collective of four influential authors: Erich Gamma, Richard Helm, Ralph Johnson, and John Vlissides, who together authored the seminal book *Design Patterns: Elements of Reusable Object-Oriented Software*. Their collaboration marked a pivotal moment in software engineering, as it introduced a systematic approach to software design, fostering a deeper understanding of object-oriented programming principles.

The Genesis of Collaboration

The collaboration among the Gang of Four was not a mere coincidence but rather a confluence of shared interests and complementary expertise. Each member brought unique strengths to the table:

- **Erich Gamma** - His profound understanding of object-oriented design principles and practical experience in software development.

- **Richard Helm** - A specialist in software architecture who contributed insights into the structural aspects of design patterns.

- **Ralph Johnson** - Known for his work on object-oriented programming languages, he provided a theoretical foundation for the patterns discussed.

- **John Vlissides** - His background in software engineering and experience in pattern-oriented design enriched the collaborative effort.

This synergy allowed the authors to explore and document design patterns in a way that was both comprehensive and accessible, making complex ideas digestible for practitioners.

Defining Design Patterns

The GoF defined a design pattern as a solution to a recurring design problem in a given context. They identified three categories of design patterns:

1. **Creational Patterns** - Concerned with the way objects are created. They address problems related to object creation mechanisms, optimizing for flexibility and reuse. Examples include:

   - *Singleton* - Ensures a class has only one instance and provides a global point of access to it.

   - *Factory Method* - Defines an interface for creating an object but allows subclasses to alter the type of objects that will be created.

2. **Structural Patterns** - Focus on how classes and objects are composed to form larger structures. They help ensure that if one part of a system changes, the entire system doesn't need to do the same. Examples include:

   - *Adapter* - Allows incompatible interfaces to work together.

   - *Decorator* - Adds new functionality to an object without altering its structure.

3. **Behavioral Patterns** - Concerned with algorithms and the assignment of responsibilities between objects. They help in defining how objects interact and communicate with each other. Examples include:

   - *Observer* - A way of notifying change to a number of classes to ensure consistency between the classes.

   - *Strategy* - Enables selecting an algorithm's behavior at runtime.

Challenges in Collaboration

Despite their expertise, the journey was fraught with challenges. One major hurdle was achieving consensus on the definitions and classifications of patterns. Each author had different experiences and perspectives, which occasionally led to disagreements. For instance, the categorization of certain patterns as creational versus structural was often debated.

Additionally, the authors faced skepticism from the broader programming community. Many were resistant to the idea that design patterns could provide reusable solutions to common problems. The team had to invest significant effort in demonstrating the practical benefits of their work through real-world examples and case studies.

The Impact of the Gang of Four's Work

The publication of *Design Patterns* in 1994 revolutionized software development. It provided developers with a common vocabulary and a toolkit for solving design problems. The book's influence can be seen in various programming languages and frameworks that adopted design patterns as foundational elements.

The Gang of Four's work also sparked a movement towards the adoption of best practices in software engineering. It encouraged developers to think critically about design and to prioritize maintainability and scalability in their code.

Conclusion

In conclusion, the collaborative efforts of the Gang of Four not only resulted in a landmark publication but also laid the groundwork for a paradigm shift in software design. Their ability to combine their individual strengths and navigate the complexities of collaboration resulted in a resource that continues to be invaluable to software engineers today. The legacy of their work is evident in the widespread adoption of design patterns, which remain a cornerstone of modern software architecture.

Documenting the Gang of Four Patterns

The process of research and analysis

The journey towards documenting the Gang of Four patterns was not merely a linear path; it was a complex tapestry woven from rigorous research, collaborative brainstorming, and iterative analysis. The authors—Erich Gamma, Richard Helm, Ralph Johnson, and John Vlissides—collectively known as the "Gang of Four" (GoF), embarked on this endeavor with a clear vision: to distill the essence of object-oriented design into comprehensible and reusable patterns.

Initial Research Framework

The initial phase of research involved an extensive literature review of existing software design methodologies. The GoF meticulously examined various programming paradigms, including procedural programming, structured programming, and early object-oriented approaches. This foundational research was critical in identifying gaps and opportunities within the existing body of knowledge.

The authors utilized a systematic approach to categorize their findings, focusing on the following key aspects:

- **Identification of Common Problems**: They began by cataloging recurring problems faced by developers in software design. This involved analyzing case studies and real-world applications where design issues frequently arose.

- **Understanding Solutions**: For each identified problem, the team sought to understand the solutions that had been previously proposed. This required diving deep into the existing literature and engaging with the software development community to gather insights.

- **Pattern Formation**: The ultimate goal was to formulate design patterns that encapsulated these solutions in a way that was both accessible and applicable to a wide range of programming scenarios.

Collaborative Analysis and Synthesis

Once the groundwork was laid, the GoF engaged in a series of brainstorming sessions to synthesize their findings into cohesive design patterns. This collaborative effort was marked by intense discussions, debates, and critical evaluations of each proposed pattern. The following methodologies were employed:

1. **Pattern Identification**: Each member of the group brought their unique perspective, leading to the identification of numerous potential patterns. They utilized whiteboard sessions to visualize relationships between problems and solutions, fostering a creative environment.

2. **Pattern Definition**: After identifying a pattern, the next step was to define it rigorously. This included specifying the pattern's name, purpose, applicability, structure, and consequences. A typical pattern description followed a format that included:

    - **Name**: A descriptive title that encapsulates the essence of the pattern.
    - **Intent**: A statement of what the pattern does and why it is useful.
    - **Motivation**: A scenario illustrating the problem and how the pattern can provide a solution.

- **Structure**: A visual representation, often in the form of UML diagrams, to depict the pattern's components and their relationships.
- **Participants**: A description of the classes and/or objects involved in the pattern.
- **Collaborations**: How the participants collaborate to fulfill the pattern's intent.
- **Consequences**: The results and trade-offs of using the pattern.

3. **Validation through Real-World Examples**: The GoF sought to validate their patterns by applying them to real-world scenarios. They examined existing software projects and identified instances where the patterns could be effectively implemented. This empirical approach not only strengthened their arguments but also provided concrete examples that could be shared with the programming community.

Challenges Encountered

The process of research and analysis was not without its challenges. The GoF faced skepticism from some quarters regarding the relevance of design patterns. Critics argued that patterns could lead to over-engineering and unnecessary complexity in software design. To counter these concerns, the authors focused on demonstrating the practical benefits of their patterns through case studies and practical applications.

Additionally, the group encountered difficulties in achieving consensus on certain patterns. Disparate opinions on the applicability of specific patterns led to intense discussions, highlighting the subjective nature of design choices in software development. However, these debates ultimately enriched the final work, leading to a more robust and nuanced understanding of design patterns.

Conclusion

In conclusion, the process of research and analysis that culminated in the creation of the Gang of Four design patterns was a multifaceted endeavor. It involved thorough literature reviews, collaborative brainstorming, rigorous validation, and navigating challenges inherent in the field of software design. The resulting patterns have since become foundational elements in object-oriented programming, illustrating the power of collective intellectual effort in addressing complex design problems. The legacy of the GoF continues to inspire and guide developers, proving that well-structured patterns can indeed transform the landscape of software engineering.

Behind the scenes of co-authorship

The journey of co-authoring the seminal work on design patterns, *Design Patterns: Elements of Reusable Object-Oriented Software*, was not merely an academic endeavor; it was a confluence of ideas, collaboration, and the occasional clash of egos. Erich Gamma, alongside his colleagues Richard Helm, Ralph Johnson, and John Vlissides—collectively known as the "Gang of Four" (GoF)—embarked on a mission that would fundamentally reshape software engineering.

The Collaborative Process

The co-authorship process was characterized by a series of intense discussions and brainstorming sessions. Each member of the GoF brought unique perspectives and expertise to the table, which enriched the content of the book. Gamma, known for his meticulous attention to detail, often took the lead in structuring the patterns and ensuring clarity in their presentation. The collaborative dynamic was both a strength and a challenge; while it fostered creativity, it also required navigating differing opinions on the best way to articulate complex concepts.

Challenges Faced

One of the primary challenges in co-authoring such a pivotal work was achieving a cohesive voice throughout the text. Each author had their own writing style, and reconciling these differences required significant effort. Gamma and his colleagues engaged in several rounds of revisions, often debating the nuances of terminology and the implications of various design choices. For instance, the team grappled with how to effectively communicate the concept of design patterns to an audience that ranged from novice programmers to seasoned developers.

Moreover, the GoF faced the challenge of selecting which patterns to include. With a plethora of design patterns emerging from the burgeoning field of object-oriented programming, prioritizing which to feature in their book was a daunting task. They needed to ensure that the chosen patterns were not only relevant but also illustrative of broader principles in software design.

Theoretical Underpinnings

At the heart of their collaboration was a shared theoretical foundation rooted in object-oriented principles. The GoF drew heavily on established theories in software engineering, such as the principles of encapsulation, inheritance, and polymorphism.

These principles served as a framework for understanding how design patterns could enhance software reusability and maintainability.

The authors adopted a systematic approach to documenting the patterns, which included the following components:

- **Pattern Name:** A descriptive name that conveys the essence of the pattern.

- **Intent:** A statement that explains what the pattern does and its purpose.

- **Motivation:** A scenario that illustrates a problem that the pattern addresses.

- **Applicability:** Situations where the pattern can be applied effectively.

- **Structure:** A visual representation of the pattern, often using UML diagrams.

- **Participants:** The classes and/or objects involved in the pattern.

- **Collaboration:** How the participants interact to carry out their responsibilities.

- **Consequences:** The trade-offs and potential impacts of using the pattern.

This structured approach not only provided clarity but also facilitated easier understanding and implementation of the patterns in real-world applications.

Real-World Examples

To ground their theories in practical application, the GoF incorporated real-world examples that demonstrated the effectiveness of each design pattern. For instance, the *Observer Pattern* was illustrated through a scenario involving a weather station that notifies multiple display elements of changes in weather conditions. This example highlighted the pattern's utility in creating a decoupled system where observers can be added or removed without altering the subject's code.

Another notable example was the *Factory Method Pattern*, which was explained using a scenario involving the creation of different types of products in a manufacturing system. This example served to illustrate the benefits of encapsulating object creation, promoting flexibility and scalability in software design.

The Legacy of Co-Authorship

The collaborative effort culminated in a publication that not only earned acclaim but also established a new lexicon within the software development community. The GoF's work laid the groundwork for future explorations into design patterns, inspiring countless programmers to adopt these principles in their own projects.

In retrospect, the behind-the-scenes dynamics of co-authorship were instrumental in shaping the final product. The interplay of diverse ideas, rigorous debate, and a shared commitment to excellence forged a legacy that continues to influence software engineering today. The Gang of Four's journey exemplifies how collaboration can lead to groundbreaking innovation, transforming individual contributions into a collective masterpiece that resonates across generations of programmers.

Controversies surrounding credit and recognition

The journey of design patterns, while groundbreaking, was not without its share of controversies, particularly regarding credit and recognition. The collaborative nature of the work done by the "Gang of Four" (GoF) in the seminal book *Design Patterns: Elements of Reusable Object-Oriented Software* has led to ongoing debates about authorship and the rightful acknowledgment of contributions.

The Nature of Collaboration

The GoF, consisting of Erich Gamma, Richard Helm, Ralph Johnson, and John Vlissides, worked closely together to distill decades of software engineering experience into a coherent framework of design patterns. This collaboration, while enriching, posed challenges in attributing specific ideas to individual contributors. The collective nature of their work led to a blending of ideas, making it difficult to delineate who should receive credit for specific patterns.

Ethical Implications

The ethical implications of credit in collaborative works are profound. In academic and professional settings, proper attribution is essential not only for individual recognition but also for the integrity of the field. The GoF faced scrutiny over how they presented their contributions, with some critics arguing that the collaborative nature of their work obscured the individual efforts that led to the creation of specific design patterns. This debate raises questions about the fairness of collective authorship and its impact on the recognition of individual contributors in the software development community.

Examples of Controversy

One notable example of controversy arose from the *Observer* pattern, which was initially described in the context of event handling in graphical user interfaces. While the concept had been utilized in various forms by multiple authors prior to the GoF's publication, the GoF's formalization of the pattern brought it into mainstream discourse. Critics argued that the GoF's work overshadowed earlier contributions, leading to a perception that they were the originators of the idea. This situation exemplifies the complexities of intellectual property in collaborative environments, where the lines between original thought and collective advancement can become blurred.

Another instance involves the *Singleton* pattern, which has been a topic of debate regarding its implementation and necessity. While the GoF popularized the pattern, it has faced criticism for promoting a design that can lead to poor software architecture if misused. This criticism often extends to the authors themselves, as some argue that the GoF's endorsement of the Singleton pattern contributed to its widespread adoption without sufficient cautionary guidance.

Recognition in Academia and Industry

In academia, the GoF's work is often cited as a foundational text in software engineering curricula. However, the emphasis on the collective authorship can sometimes overshadow the individual contributions of its members. This has led to a situation where students and emerging programmers may not fully appreciate the distinct roles played by each member of the GoF in shaping the field of design patterns.

In the industry, the recognition of design patterns has led to a proliferation of resources, including books, courses, and online tutorials. However, many of these resources fail to adequately credit the GoF and their contributions. This lack of recognition can perpetuate the myth that design patterns are a universally accepted concept that emerged organically, rather than the result of specific individuals' efforts and insights.

The Path Forward

To navigate the complexities of credit and recognition in collaborative works, it is crucial for the software development community to foster a culture of acknowledgment. This includes explicitly citing the contributions of individuals within collaborative projects and ensuring that educational resources reflect the historical context of design patterns.

Furthermore, as the field of software engineering continues to evolve, it is essential to engage in ongoing discussions about the ethical implications of authorship and recognition. By addressing these controversies, the community can honor the contributions of pioneers like Erich Gamma and his colleagues while also encouraging future innovation in software design.

In conclusion, the controversies surrounding credit and recognition in the context of design patterns highlight the intricate dynamics of collaboration in the software development field. As we continue to build upon the foundation laid by the GoF, it is imperative to recognize and celebrate the individual contributions that have shaped our understanding of design patterns and their application in software engineering.

Impact and Legacy

The worldwide adoption of design patterns

How design patterns changed the software industry

The introduction of design patterns into the software industry marked a pivotal moment that transformed the way developers approached software design and architecture. Before the emergence of design patterns, software development often resembled a chaotic endeavor, with developers relying on ad-hoc solutions and personal heuristics to tackle complex problems. This lack of standardization led to inefficiencies, increased maintenance costs, and a steep learning curve for new developers.

Design patterns provided a structured approach to software design, offering reusable solutions to common problems encountered in software development. They encapsulated best practices and distilled the collective wisdom of experienced software engineers into a set of guidelines that could be applied across various programming languages and frameworks. The impact of design patterns can be seen in several key areas:

Standardization of Solutions

One of the most significant contributions of design patterns was the standardization of solutions to recurring problems. By categorizing these solutions into recognizable patterns, developers could communicate more effectively and share knowledge across teams. For example, the **Singleton** pattern, which restricts a class to a single instance, became a widely accepted solution for managing global state in applications. This standardization reduced the ambiguity around how to implement certain functionalities, leading to more consistent codebases and improved collaboration among developers.

Enhanced Code Maintainability

Design patterns also played a crucial role in enhancing the maintainability of software systems. With a clear understanding of design patterns, developers could create systems that were modular and easier to understand. For instance, the **Observer** pattern allows for a clean separation of concerns by defining a one-to-many dependency between objects, enabling changes to one object to automatically notify and update others. This decoupling of components means that changes can be made with minimal impact on the overall system, thereby reducing the risk of introducing bugs during maintenance.

Facilitating Agile Development

The rise of agile methodologies in the software industry coincided with the adoption of design patterns. Agile development emphasizes iterative progress, collaboration, and responsiveness to change. Design patterns align well with these principles by providing flexible and adaptable solutions that can evolve alongside the project. For example, the **Strategy** pattern allows for the selection of algorithms at runtime, making it easier to adapt to changing requirements without overhauling the entire system architecture.

Real-World Examples

The influence of design patterns can be observed in many successful software applications. For instance, the Model-View-Controller (MVC) architecture, which separates an application into three interconnected components, is heavily influenced by design patterns. Frameworks such as Ruby on Rails and AngularJS have adopted the MVC pattern, allowing developers to build scalable and maintainable web applications efficiently.

Another notable example is the use of the **Decorator** pattern in graphical user interface (GUI) frameworks, where it allows developers to add new functionality to objects dynamically. This pattern is prevalent in Java's Swing library, enabling the creation of complex user interfaces with minimal code duplication.

Conclusion

In conclusion, the introduction of design patterns revolutionized the software industry by providing developers with a common language and a set of best practices to tackle complex design challenges. The standardization of solutions, enhanced maintainability, and alignment with agile methodologies have made design patterns an indispensable tool in the software development toolkit. As the industry continues to evolve, the principles of design patterns will remain relevant, guiding developers in creating robust, scalable, and maintainable software systems.

Real-life examples of design patterns in action

Design patterns, as established by Erich Gamma and his colleagues, have become integral to the software engineering landscape. They offer solutions to common problems faced by developers, enabling them to create more efficient, maintainable, and scalable software. In this section, we will explore several real-life examples of design patterns in action, illustrating their significance and practical applications in various domains.

1. The Singleton Pattern in Database Connections

One of the most widely used design patterns is the Singleton pattern, which ensures that a class has only one instance and provides a global point of access to it. This is particularly useful in scenarios where a single point of control is required, such as managing database connections.

```
class DatabaseConnection {
private:
    static DatabaseConnection* instance;
    DatabaseConnection() {} // Private constructor

public:
    static DatabaseConnection* getInstance() {
        if (instance == nullptr) {
            instance = new DatabaseConnection();
        }
        return\index{return} instance\index{instance};
    }
};
```

In this example, the 'DatabaseConnection' class can only be instantiated once. Any subsequent calls to 'getInstance()' will return the same instance, ensuring that all parts of the application share the same database connection. This pattern not only reduces resource consumption but also simplifies the management of connections.

2. The Observer Pattern in User Interface Development

The Observer pattern is another prominent design pattern, particularly in the development of user interfaces. It defines a one-to-many dependency between objects so that when one object changes state, all its dependents are notified and updated automatically. This pattern is commonly used in event-driven programming.

Consider a simple application where a user can subscribe to updates from a news agency. The 'NewsAgency' class acts as the subject, while various 'Subscriber' classes act as observers.

```
class NewsAgency {
private:
    std::vector<Subscriber*> subscribers;

public:
    void subscribe(Subscriber* subscriber) {
        subscribers.push_back(subscriber);
    }

    void notifySubscribers() {
        for (auto\& subscriber : subscribers) {
            subscriber->update();
        }
    }

    void publishNews() {
        // Publish news and notify subscribers
        notifySubscribers();
    }
};
```

In this scenario, when the 'NewsAgency' publishes news, it automatically notifies all subscribed users. This decouples the subjects from their observers, allowing for greater flexibility and scalability in the application.

3. The Factory Method Pattern in E-commerce Applications

In e-commerce applications, the Factory Method pattern is often employed to create objects without specifying the exact class of object that will be created. This is particularly useful in scenarios where the type of object to be created can vary based on user input or other conditions.

For instance, an online store might offer different types of products, such as electronics and clothing. The 'ProductFactory' class can be designed to create products based on the type specified by the user.

```cpp
class Product {
public:
    virtual void create() = 0;
};

class Electronics : public Product {
public:
    void create() override {
        // Create electronics product
    }
};

class Clothing : public Product {
public:
    void create() override {
        // Create clothing product
    }
};

class ProductFactory {
public:
    static Product* createProduct(const std::string\& type) {
        if (type == ``Electronics") {
            return new Electronics();
        } else if (type == ``Clothing") {
            return new Clothing();
        }
        return nullptr;
    }
};
```

This pattern allows the application to easily extend its product offerings without modifying existing code, adhering to the Open/Closed Principle of software design.

4. The Strategy Pattern in Payment Processing

The Strategy pattern is a behavioral design pattern that enables selecting an algorithm's behavior at runtime. This is particularly useful in payment processing systems, where different payment methods can be employed based on user preference.

Consider an e-commerce application that supports multiple payment methods such as credit cards, PayPal, and cryptocurrency. The 'PaymentStrategy' interface defines a method for processing payments, and concrete implementations provide the specific payment logic.

```cpp
class PaymentStrategy {
public:
    virtual void pay(double amount) = 0;
};

class CreditCardPayment : public PaymentStrategy {
public:
    void pay(double amount) override {
        // Process credit card payment
    }
};

class PayPalPayment : public PaymentStrategy {
public:
    void pay(double amount) override {
        // Process PayPal payment
    }
};

class ShoppingCart {
private:
    PaymentStrategy* paymentStrategy;

public:
    void setPaymentStrategy(PaymentStrategy* strategy) {
        paymentStrategy = strategy;
    }
```

```
    void checkout(double amount) {
        paymentStrategy->pay(amount);
    }
};
```

In this example, the 'ShoppingCart' class can dynamically change its payment method based on user selection, promoting flexibility and maintainability.

5. The Adapter Pattern in Legacy System Integration

The Adapter pattern is a structural design pattern that allows incompatible interfaces to work together. This is particularly useful when integrating legacy systems with new applications.

Imagine a scenario where a new application needs to communicate with an older system that uses a different interface. The 'Adapter' class can be created to bridge the gap between the two systems.

```
class LegacySystem {
public:
    void legacyRequest() {
        // Legacy system request
    }
};

class NewSystem {
public:
    virtual void newRequest() = 0;
};

class Adapter : public NewSystem {
private:
    LegacySystem* legacySystem;

public:
    Adapter(LegacySystem* system) : legacySystem(system) {}

    void newRequest() override {
        legacySystem->legacyRequest();
    }
};
```

By using the Adapter pattern, the new system can seamlessly interact with the legacy system without requiring extensive modifications to either system.

Conclusion

These real-life examples illustrate the versatility and practicality of design patterns in software development. By applying these patterns, developers can solve common problems effectively, enhance code reusability, and improve maintainability. The principles established by Erich Gamma and his colleagues continue to resonate in the programming community, guiding developers towards creating robust and scalable software solutions.

The enduring relevance of design patterns

Design patterns have established themselves as a cornerstone of software development, transcending the realms of mere theory to become practical tools that developers rely on daily. Their enduring relevance can be attributed to several key factors, including their ability to facilitate communication, enhance code reusability, and provide solutions to recurring problems in software design.

Facilitating Communication

One of the primary advantages of design patterns is their role in fostering clear communication among developers. By providing a shared vocabulary, design patterns enable programmers to articulate complex design concepts succinctly. For instance, when a developer mentions the `Observer` pattern, colleagues can immediately grasp the intended design without needing extensive explanations. This shared understanding streamlines collaboration and reduces the cognitive load associated with deciphering intricate codebases.

Enhancing Code Reusability

Design patterns promote code reusability, a principle that stands at the heart of efficient software development. By encapsulating best practices into reusable templates, developers can avoid redundancy and minimize the likelihood of introducing errors. For example, the `Factory Method` pattern allows for the creation of objects without specifying the exact class of object that will be created. This abstraction not only simplifies code maintenance but also enhances adaptability, as new classes can be introduced without altering existing code.

Providing Solutions to Recurring Problems

Design patterns serve as proven solutions to common problems that arise during software development. The `Singleton` pattern, for instance, addresses the need for a single instance of a class while providing a global access point. This pattern is particularly useful in scenarios such as database connections, where multiple instances may lead to resource contention and inconsistent states. By implementing the `Singleton` pattern, developers can ensure that only one instance of the class is created, thereby maintaining consistency and optimizing resource usage.

Real-World Applications

The relevance of design patterns is further illustrated by their widespread adoption in real-world applications. Consider the use of the `Decorator` pattern in graphical user interface (GUI) frameworks. This pattern allows developers to dynamically add responsibilities to objects without modifying their structure. For example, a basic text component can be enhanced with scrolling, borders, or background colors by wrapping it in decorator classes. This flexibility not only promotes code modularity but also enables developers to create rich user experiences with minimal effort.

Moreover, the `Strategy` pattern exemplifies how design patterns can enhance algorithmic flexibility. By defining a family of algorithms and encapsulating each one, the `Strategy` pattern allows clients to choose the algorithm at runtime. This is particularly advantageous in scenarios where the optimal algorithm may vary based on user input or environmental factors, such as sorting algorithms in a data processing application.

Adapting to New Paradigms

As technology evolves, so too does the landscape of software development. Design patterns have shown remarkable adaptability, integrating seamlessly with emerging paradigms such as functional programming and microservices architecture. For instance, the principles behind the `Command` pattern, which encapsulates a request as an object, can be effectively applied in event-driven architectures, allowing for greater scalability and flexibility in handling asynchronous operations.

Furthermore, the rise of cloud computing and distributed systems has necessitated the reevaluation of traditional design patterns. Patterns such as `Circuit Breaker` and `Event Sourcing` have emerged to address the challenges posed by network latency and service failures in distributed environments. These patterns not only enhance system resilience but also align with modern development practices, ensuring that design patterns remain relevant in the face of rapid technological advancements.

Conclusion

In conclusion, the enduring relevance of design patterns lies in their ability to facilitate communication, enhance code reusability, and provide robust solutions to recurring problems. Their application in real-world scenarios, coupled with their adaptability to new paradigms, underscores their significance in the ever-evolving field of software development. As programmers continue to navigate the complexities of modern applications, design patterns will undoubtedly remain an invaluable resource, guiding them toward efficient and effective solutions.

Erich Gamma's contributions beyond design patterns

Architectural Patterns and Frameworks

Architectural patterns represent a high-level solution to a recurring design problem in software architecture. They provide a blueprint for designing systems and are crucial in defining the structure of software applications. Unlike design patterns, which focus on specific problems in the implementation phase, architectural patterns address broader concerns related to the overall system architecture. This section explores the significance of architectural patterns, their common types, and frameworks that embody these patterns.

Understanding Architectural Patterns

Architectural patterns help in organizing code, improving maintainability, and enhancing scalability. They serve as a guide for developers to create robust systems that can adapt to changing requirements. By employing architectural patterns, developers can avoid common pitfalls and create a solid foundation for their applications.

Some common architectural patterns include:

- **Layered Pattern:** This pattern organizes the system into layers, where each layer has specific responsibilities. The most common layers include presentation, business logic, and data access. This separation of concerns allows for easier maintenance and testing.

+ **Client-Server Pattern:** This pattern divides the system into two parts: the client, which requests services, and the server, which provides those services. This model is prevalent in web applications where the client is the browser and the server hosts the application.

+ **Microservices Architecture:** This modern architectural style structures an application as a collection of loosely coupled services. Each service is independently deployable and can be developed in different programming languages. This promotes scalability and agility in development.

+ **Event-Driven Architecture:** This pattern focuses on the production, detection, consumption of, and reaction to events. It is particularly useful in systems that require high responsiveness and scalability, such as real-time applications.

The Role of Frameworks

Frameworks are essential tools that implement architectural patterns and provide developers with a pre-defined structure to work within. They encapsulate best practices and design principles, allowing developers to focus on building features rather than worrying about the underlying architecture.

For instance, consider the following frameworks that embody architectural patterns:

+ **Spring Framework:** This framework is widely used in Java applications and follows the layered architecture pattern. It provides extensive support for building enterprise-level applications, including dependency injection, aspect-oriented programming, and transaction management.

+ **Django:** This Python web framework follows the Model-View-Template (MVT) architectural pattern, which is a variation of the MVC pattern. Django simplifies web development by providing built-in components such as authentication, ORM, and admin interfaces.

+ **Angular:** A popular framework for building single-page applications (SPAs), Angular adopts a component-based architecture. This allows developers to create reusable components that manage their own state and rendering, enhancing modularity and maintainability.

Challenges in Architectural Design

Despite the advantages, implementing architectural patterns and frameworks is not without challenges. Some common issues include:

- **Overengineering:** Developers may be tempted to adopt complex patterns and frameworks, leading to unnecessary complexity in simple applications. It is crucial to evaluate whether the chosen architecture aligns with the project requirements.

- **Performance Overhead:** Some frameworks may introduce performance overhead due to their abstraction layers. Developers must carefully assess the trade-offs between ease of use and system performance.

- **Integration Difficulties:** When integrating different architectural patterns or frameworks, compatibility issues may arise. Ensuring that components work seamlessly together requires thorough planning and testing.

Real-Life Examples

Real-life applications of architectural patterns can be observed in various domains. For instance:

- **E-Commerce Platforms:** Many e-commerce systems utilize a microservices architecture to handle different functionalities such as user management, product catalog, and payment processing. This allows teams to work independently on different services, accelerating development and deployment.

- **Social Media Applications:** Event-driven architecture is commonly used in social media platforms to handle user interactions and notifications in real time. By reacting to events, these applications can provide a responsive user experience.

- **Banking Systems:** Traditional banking applications often employ layered architecture to separate concerns such as user interface, business logic, and data access. This helps in managing complex business rules while ensuring security and compliance.

Conclusion

Architectural patterns and frameworks are vital components in the software development process. They provide developers with proven solutions to common architectural challenges, promoting the creation of scalable, maintainable, and efficient systems. By understanding and effectively applying these patterns, programmers can significantly enhance their software design capabilities, paving the way for innovative and robust applications. As the software landscape continues to evolve, the importance of architectural patterns will only grow, making them an essential area of study for aspiring programmers and seasoned professionals alike.

Leadership in the software development community

Erich Gamma's influence extends far beyond the pages of his seminal work on design patterns; he has played a pivotal role in shaping the culture and practices of the software development community. His leadership is characterized by a commitment to collaboration, innovation, and mentorship, which has inspired countless developers and shaped the trajectory of software engineering.

Championing Collaboration

One of Gamma's most significant contributions to the software development community is his advocacy for collaboration. His work with the *Gang of Four*, which included Richard Helm, Ralph Johnson, and John Vlissides, exemplifies the power of teamwork. Together, they crafted a comprehensive guide to design patterns that has become a cornerstone of object-oriented programming. This collaborative effort not only produced a seminal text but also set a precedent for how software development could be approached as a collective endeavor.

Gamma's belief in collaboration is further reflected in his involvement with open-source projects. He has often emphasized the importance of community-driven development, where ideas can be freely exchanged and improved upon. For instance, his contributions to the *Eclipse* IDE not only enhanced the platform but also encouraged a community of developers to contribute their own innovations, fostering an environment of shared knowledge and collective progress.

Mentorship and Education

Gamma's leadership is also evident in his role as a mentor to aspiring programmers and developers. He has consistently sought to share his knowledge through teaching and speaking engagements. His lectures at conferences, workshops, and universities have inspired a new generation of software engineers to embrace the principles of design patterns and object-oriented programming.

Furthermore, Gamma has been involved in various educational initiatives aimed at improving programming curricula. He understands that the future of software development relies on the education of young programmers. By advocating for a curriculum that emphasizes design patterns and best practices, he has helped shape the educational landscape, ensuring that upcoming developers are well-equipped to tackle complex software challenges.

Thought Leadership and Innovation

As a thought leader, Gamma has been at the forefront of discussions regarding the evolution of software development practices. He has not only contributed to the theoretical underpinnings of programming but has also been an active participant in the practical applications of these theories. His insights into software architecture and design have influenced industry standards and practices.

For example, Gamma's work on the *Model-View-Controller* (MVC) architecture has had a lasting impact on web development. The MVC pattern, which separates the application logic from the user interface, has become a fundamental design principle that many modern frameworks, such as Ruby on Rails and Angular, are built upon. This separation of concerns not only enhances code maintainability but also fosters a more organized approach to software development.

Addressing Industry Challenges

Gamma's leadership also involves addressing the challenges faced by the software development community. He has been vocal about the need for improved software quality and maintainability. In an era where software systems are becoming increasingly complex, Gamma has advocated for practices that emphasize clean code, thorough documentation, and robust testing methodologies.

His emphasis on design patterns can be seen as a response to the common pitfalls in software design, such as code duplication and tight coupling. By promoting the use of design patterns, Gamma has provided developers with tools to create more flexible and maintainable codebases. This proactive approach to problem-solving has not only benefited individual developers but has also contributed to the overall health of the software industry.

Inspiring a Culture of Excellence

Gamma's leadership style fosters a culture of excellence within the software development community. He encourages developers to strive for high standards in their work, promoting the idea that software development is not just a technical endeavor but also an art form. By sharing his own experiences and challenges, he has shown that the path to excellence is often fraught with obstacles, but perseverance and dedication can lead to remarkable achievements.

Through his leadership, Gamma has established a legacy that transcends his individual contributions. He has inspired a community of developers to embrace collaboration, innovation, and continuous learning. His commitment to excellence serves as a guiding principle for many, encouraging them to push the boundaries of what is possible in software development.

In conclusion, Erich Gamma's leadership in the software development community is marked by his collaborative spirit, dedication to mentorship, and commitment to addressing industry challenges. His contributions have not only shaped the principles of software design but have also inspired a culture of excellence that continues to influence developers around the world. As the software landscape evolves, Gamma's insights and leadership will undoubtedly remain a beacon for future generations of programmers.

Inspiring the next generation of programmers

Erich Gamma's impact on the field of software development extends far beyond his contributions to design patterns; it resonates profoundly within the hearts and minds of aspiring programmers around the world. His journey serves as a beacon of inspiration, illuminating the path for those who wish to follow in his footsteps. This section explores how Gamma's work, philosophy, and mentorship have inspired the next generation of programmers, fostering creativity, innovation, and a deeper understanding of software engineering.

The Power of Mentorship

One of the most significant ways in which Erich Gamma has inspired upcoming programmers is through his commitment to mentorship. Understanding the challenges faced by novice developers, Gamma has often taken on the role of a mentor, guiding young minds through the complexities of programming. His approach emphasizes not just technical skills but also the importance of critical thinking and problem-solving.

For instance, Gamma has been known to participate in various workshops and conferences, where he shares his insights on object-oriented programming and design patterns. During these sessions, he encourages participants to engage in hands-on coding exercises, fostering an environment where learning is both practical and enjoyable. By sharing real-world examples and case studies, he demonstrates how design patterns can be applied to solve common problems, thereby equipping the next generation with the tools they need to succeed.

Promoting a Growth Mindset

Gamma's philosophy promotes a growth mindset, which is crucial for aspiring programmers. He believes that programming is not merely a set of skills to be mastered but a journey of continuous learning and adaptation. This perspective encourages young developers to embrace challenges and view failures as opportunities for growth.

For example, during a coding bootcamp, Gamma might challenge participants to refactor existing code using design patterns. This exercise not only reinforces their understanding of the patterns but also teaches them resilience in the face of difficulty. By encouraging experimentation and iterative improvement, Gamma instills a sense of confidence in his mentees, empowering them to tackle increasingly complex projects.

Fostering Creativity and Innovation

In addition to technical skills, Gamma emphasizes the importance of creativity in programming. He encourages young developers to think outside the box and explore innovative solutions to problems. This creative approach is evident in his own work, where he has consistently pushed the boundaries of software design.

A notable example of this is the development of the `Observer` pattern, which allows for a flexible and dynamic way to handle events in software applications. By demonstrating how this pattern can be used to create responsive user interfaces, Gamma inspires programmers to consider how design choices can lead to more engaging and user-friendly applications.

Engaging with the Community

Gamma's influence extends into the broader programming community, where he actively engages with developers through forums, online courses, and open-source projects. His willingness to share knowledge and collaborate with others has created a culture of openness and support among programmers.

Through platforms like GitHub, Gamma has contributed to numerous open-source projects, providing young developers with the opportunity to learn from real-world codebases. By participating in these projects, aspiring programmers can see firsthand how design patterns are implemented in practical scenarios, reinforcing their understanding and encouraging them to contribute their own ideas.

Real-World Applications and Case Studies

To further inspire the next generation, Gamma often shares real-world applications of design patterns in various industries. For example, in the realm of game development, he discusses how the `Factory Method` pattern can be utilized to streamline the creation of game objects, allowing for greater flexibility and scalability. By presenting such case studies, he illustrates the tangible benefits of applying design patterns, motivating young programmers to adopt these practices in their own work.

Conclusion

In conclusion, Erich Gamma's role in inspiring the next generation of programmers is multifaceted. Through mentorship, the promotion of a growth mindset, encouragement of creativity, community engagement, and real-world applications, he has created a lasting legacy that continues to influence and empower aspiring developers. As they navigate the complexities of software engineering, these young minds carry forward the ideals and principles that Gamma has championed, ensuring that his impact will be felt for years to come. By nurturing a new generation of programmers, Gamma not only shapes the future of software development but also fosters a community that values collaboration, innovation, and lifelong learning.

Personal Life and Reflections

Balancing work and personal life

Family and relationships

Erich Gamma's journey into the world of programming did not occur in isolation; it was profoundly influenced by the familial bonds that shaped his early years. Growing up in Zurich, Switzerland, Gamma was surrounded by a nurturing environment that fostered curiosity and innovation. His parents, both educators, instilled in him the values of hard work, integrity, and the pursuit of knowledge. This foundational support played a crucial role in his development as a programmer.

The Influence of Family

Gamma's family dynamics were characterized by open communication and encouragement. His father, a mathematics teacher, often engaged him in discussions about logical reasoning and problem-solving from a young age. This early exposure to analytical thinking laid the groundwork for Gamma's future endeavors in computer science. His mother, a literature teacher, introduced him to the beauty of language and storytelling, which would later influence his ability to articulate complex programming concepts clearly.

The balance between the arts and sciences in his upbringing provided Gamma with a unique perspective. He learned to appreciate the creativity involved in coding, viewing it not merely as a technical skill but as a form of expression. This holistic approach to learning helped him cultivate a well-rounded intellect, essential for innovation in software development.

Relationships and Mentorship

As Gamma navigated through his formative years, he formed significant relationships with mentors who would guide him along his path. One notable figure was his high school computer science teacher, who recognized Gamma's potential early on. This mentor not only introduced him to programming languages but also encouraged him to participate in coding competitions, where he honed his skills and discovered the thrill of problem-solving in a competitive environment.

These relationships extended beyond formal education. Gamma was part of a close-knit group of friends who shared his passion for technology. They often gathered to discuss programming challenges, share insights, and collaborate on projects. This camaraderie created a supportive network that nurtured his talents and fueled his ambition to excel in the field of software development.

Balancing Personal Life and Career

As Gamma's career progressed, the demands of his professional life began to intensify. Balancing work and personal life became increasingly challenging, particularly as he gained recognition in the programming community. However, he remained committed to maintaining strong relationships with his family and friends. Gamma often emphasized the importance of carving out time for loved ones, believing that these connections were vital for personal well-being and professional success.

One of the strategies he employed was to set boundaries around his work schedule. Gamma would allocate specific time blocks for family activities, ensuring that he was present for important events and milestones. This intentional approach allowed him to nurture his relationships while pursuing his career goals. He often reflected on how these moments of connection provided him with the motivation and inspiration needed to tackle complex programming challenges.

The Role of Family in Achievements

Gamma's family played a significant role in his achievements, serving as a source of encouragement during challenging times. His spouse, who shared his interest in technology, was particularly supportive of his endeavors. Together, they navigated the ups and downs of his career, celebrating successes and providing comfort during setbacks. This partnership exemplified the idea that personal relationships can be a source of strength in the pursuit of professional excellence.

Moreover, Gamma's children have also been a source of inspiration for him. He often speaks about how their curiosity and enthusiasm for learning remind him of his own childhood experiences with coding. This generational connection has led him to become more involved in initiatives aimed at encouraging young people to explore programming, reinforcing the idea that fostering a love for technology is a family affair.

Conclusion

In summary, Erich Gamma's family and relationships have been integral to his journey as a programmer. The values instilled by his parents, the mentorship he received, and the support from his loved ones have all contributed to his success. By prioritizing these connections, Gamma has not only managed to balance the demands of his career but has also cultivated a rich personal life that continues to inspire his work. As he reflects on his journey, he acknowledges that the love and support of family have been pivotal in shaping the programmer he is today.

Coping with the demands of fame and success

The journey to fame and success is often a double-edged sword, particularly in the fast-paced world of technology. For Erich Gamma, the co-author of the influential "Design Patterns" book, navigating the waters of recognition and acclaim presented unique challenges. This section delves into the complexities of coping with fame, exploring the psychological and social implications, as well as practical strategies employed by Gamma to maintain balance in his life.

The Psychological Toll of Fame

Fame can lead to heightened expectations and pressure, creating a psychological burden that many successful individuals face. Erich Gamma, celebrated for his contributions to software engineering, experienced the weight of public scrutiny. The phenomenon known as *impostor syndrome* often plagues high achievers, where individuals doubt their accomplishments and fear being exposed as a "fraud." Gamma, despite his expertise, occasionally grappled with self-doubt, questioning whether he truly deserved the accolades.

The pressures of fame can also lead to stress and anxiety. Research indicates that individuals in high-profile positions may experience a range of emotional challenges, including increased levels of *stress hormones* such as cortisol. This physiological response can manifest in various ways, from sleep disturbances to decreased overall well-being. Gamma's journey highlights the importance of recognizing these psychological impacts and seeking support when necessary.

Maintaining Personal Relationships

One of the significant challenges faced by those in the spotlight is the strain on personal relationships. The demands of fame can lead to a lack of time and energy for family and friends. Erich Gamma, aware of this potential pitfall, made conscious efforts to prioritize his personal life. He often emphasized the importance of maintaining strong connections with loved ones as a source of emotional support.

In his biography, Gamma reflects on the necessity of setting boundaries between work and personal life. He implemented strategies such as designated family time and unplugging from technology during significant moments. This approach not only nurtured his relationships but also provided a much-needed respite from the pressures of his professional life.

Strategies for Coping with Success

To cope with the demands of fame and success, Erich Gamma adopted several strategies that proved effective in maintaining his mental health and overall well-being. These strategies included:

- **Mindfulness and Stress Reduction:** Gamma engaged in mindfulness practices, such as meditation and yoga, which helped him stay grounded amidst the chaos of fame. Research indicates that mindfulness can reduce stress and enhance emotional regulation, allowing individuals to navigate challenges with greater resilience.

- **Continuous Learning:** Gamma maintained a commitment to lifelong learning, viewing challenges as opportunities for growth. This mindset not only fueled his passion for programming but also provided a sense of purpose beyond the accolades. Embracing a growth mindset, as outlined by psychologist Carol Dweck, can empower individuals to thrive in the face of adversity.

- **Seeking Professional Help:** Recognizing the importance of mental health, Gamma was not hesitant to seek professional guidance when needed. Therapy and counseling can offer valuable tools for coping with the emotional toll of fame, providing a safe space for individuals to process their experiences.

+ **Giving Back:** Engaging in philanthropic activities and mentoring aspiring programmers allowed Gamma to shift the focus away from himself and contribute positively to the community. This sense of purpose can alleviate feelings of isolation often associated with fame.

The Balance Between Fame and Authenticity

Ultimately, coping with fame requires a delicate balance between public persona and personal authenticity. Erich Gamma navigated this challenge by remaining true to his values and passions. He emphasized the importance of authenticity in both his personal and professional life, advocating for transparency in a field often dominated by competition and ego.

In conclusion, the demands of fame and success are multifaceted, presenting both opportunities and challenges. For Erich Gamma, coping with these demands involved a combination of psychological awareness, relationship maintenance, and proactive strategies. By prioritizing mental health and authenticity, he not only navigated the complexities of fame but also set an example for future generations of programmers. His journey serves as a reminder that success is not solely defined by accolades but by the ability to remain grounded and true to oneself amidst the whirlwind of recognition.

Lessons learned and regrets

Reflections on the design patterns journey

The journey of Erich Gamma and the development of design patterns is not just a tale of technical innovation; it is a narrative steeped in introspection, learning, and the evolution of thought within software engineering. As we delve into this reflection, we recognize that the creation and adoption of design patterns were not merely a series of decisions made in isolation but rather a confluence of experiences, challenges, and insights that shaped the landscape of programming.

Understanding the Journey

Design patterns emerged in the early 1990s as a response to the increasing complexity of software systems. The essence of a design pattern is its ability to provide a reusable solution to common problems within a given context. This concept can be formalized as follows:

$$P = \{S, C, R\} \tag{15}$$

where P represents a design pattern, S is the problem it addresses, C is the context in which it applies, and R is the resulting solution. This formalization highlights the interconnectedness of problems, contexts, and solutions in the realm of software design.

Initial Challenges and Skepticism

Despite the theoretical elegance of design patterns, their introduction was met with skepticism. Many developers were entrenched in procedural programming paradigms and viewed object-oriented principles with suspicion. The initial challenge was to illustrate the practical utility of design patterns in real-world applications.

Gamma and his colleagues faced the daunting task of overcoming this skepticism. They organized workshops and discussions to demonstrate the effectiveness of design patterns. One notable example was the implementation of the **Observer Pattern**, which allows a subject to notify multiple observers of state changes. This pattern was instrumental in the development of user interface frameworks, where it facilitated the separation of concerns and enhanced modularity.

Lessons Learned from Collaboration

The collaborative effort among the "Gang of Four"—Gamma, Richard Helm, Ralph Johnson, and John Vlissides—was pivotal in refining the concept of design patterns. Each member brought unique perspectives and expertise, enriching the discussion and leading to a more comprehensive understanding of design patterns.

Through their collaboration, they learned the importance of clear communication and shared vision. They developed a common language to articulate complex ideas, which ultimately made the patterns more accessible to the broader programming community. The experience underscored the value of teamwork in overcoming intellectual barriers and fostering innovation.

Reflections on Mistakes and Growth

As with any groundbreaking endeavor, the journey was not without its missteps. Gamma reflects on certain patterns that, while theoretically sound, proved impractical in specific contexts. For instance, the **Singleton Pattern**, which restricts a class to a single instance, often led to issues in testing and increased coupling in systems. These reflections prompted a reevaluation of certain patterns and an understanding that no solution is universally applicable.

This journey of trial and error taught Gamma and his colleagues the importance of adaptability. They recognized that design patterns should not be rigid templates but rather flexible guidelines that can be tailored to fit the needs of a particular situation. This adaptability is encapsulated in the following principle:

$$F = \{E, A\} \tag{16}$$

where F represents flexibility, E is the environment, and A is the adaptation of the pattern to that environment. This principle has since become a cornerstone of effective software design.

The Enduring Impact of Design Patterns

Reflecting on the journey, Gamma acknowledges the profound impact that design patterns have had on software engineering. They have become a lingua franca among developers, providing a shared vocabulary for discussing solutions to common problems. The adoption of design patterns has led to more maintainable, scalable, and robust software systems.

Real-life examples abound, illustrating the effectiveness of design patterns in practice. For instance, the use of the **Decorator Pattern** in graphical user interface (GUI) frameworks allows developers to add functionality to objects dynamically without altering their structure. This pattern promotes flexibility and reusability, key tenets of modern software design.

As design patterns continue to evolve, they inspire new generations of programmers to think critically about their approaches to problem-solving. The legacy of Gamma and his colleagues is not merely in the patterns themselves but in the mindset they fostered—one that encourages creativity, collaboration, and continuous improvement.

Conclusion of Reflections

In conclusion, the reflections on the design patterns journey reveal a tapestry woven from experiences, challenges, and insights. Erich Gamma's journey exemplifies the iterative nature of learning in the field of software development. The lessons learned from this journey serve as a beacon for current and future programmers, reminding them that the path to innovation is often fraught with obstacles but ultimately rewarding. As design patterns continue to influence the software industry, the journey of Erich Gamma remains a testament to the power of thoughtful design and collaboration in shaping the future of programming.

Acknowledging mistakes and embracing growth

In the journey of any great programmer, the path is seldom linear. For Erich Gamma, the co-author of the seminal work *Design Patterns: Elements of Reusable Object-Oriented Software*, acknowledging mistakes has been a crucial aspect of his growth as a programmer and a leader in the software development community. Embracing the lessons learned from these missteps has not only shaped his personal philosophy but has also influenced the broader programming landscape.

The Nature of Mistakes in Programming

Mistakes in programming can manifest in various forms, including design flaws, inefficient algorithms, and miscommunications within teams. The complexity of software systems often leads to unforeseen issues that can derail projects. For Gamma, one of the most significant lessons learned was that mistakes are not merely failures; they are opportunities for learning and improvement.

Consider the case of the initial implementation of a design pattern. The **Singleton Pattern**, for instance, was originally designed to restrict instantiation of a class to a single instance. However, early implementations often overlooked thread safety, leading to potential issues in multi-threaded environments. Gamma and his colleagues faced criticism for this oversight, which prompted them to revisit and refine their approach. The lesson learned here was the importance of rigorous testing and validation in ensuring that theoretical concepts translate effectively into practical applications.

Embracing Growth Through Reflection

Reflection is a powerful tool for personal and professional growth. Gamma often emphasizes the importance of taking a step back to analyze past decisions and their outcomes. This reflective practice allows individuals to identify patterns in their behavior and decision-making processes, leading to more informed choices in the future.

For example, in the development of the **Observer Pattern**, Gamma and his team initially struggled with the complexity of managing dependencies between objects. Through introspection, they recognized that simplifying the communication process between objects could enhance usability. This realization led to a more robust and flexible implementation of the Observer Pattern, showcasing how acknowledging a mistake can lead to innovative solutions.

The Role of Mentorship and Collaboration

Gamma's journey also highlights the importance of mentorship and collaboration in acknowledging mistakes and fostering growth. Throughout his career, he has actively sought feedback from peers and mentors, recognizing that diverse perspectives can illuminate blind spots.

In collaborative environments, mistakes often become collective learning experiences. For instance, during the development of the **Decorator Pattern**, Gamma and his colleagues encountered challenges with the implementation that initially seemed insurmountable. However, through open discussions and brainstorming sessions, the team was able to pivot their approach and ultimately create a more elegant solution. This experience reinforced Gamma's belief that collaboration not only mitigates individual errors but also enhances the overall quality of the work produced.

Cultivating a Growth Mindset

A growth mindset, as popularized by psychologist Carol Dweck, is the belief that abilities and intelligence can be developed through dedication and hard work. Gamma embodies this mindset, viewing challenges as opportunities to expand his skills and knowledge.

For instance, when faced with criticism regarding the initial reception of design patterns, Gamma chose to engage with his critics rather than retreating in defensiveness. He participated in discussions and workshops to understand the concerns of fellow programmers, which ultimately led to the refinement of the design patterns framework. This proactive approach not only improved his work but also contributed to the evolution of software engineering as a discipline.

Conclusion: The Power of Acknowledgment

In conclusion, Erich Gamma's journey underscores the significance of acknowledging mistakes and embracing growth. By viewing errors as stepping stones rather than stumbling blocks, he has cultivated a career marked by continuous learning and innovation. The programming community can benefit from adopting similar attitudes, fostering an environment where mistakes are seen as valuable lessons that drive progress.

As Gamma continues to explore new frontiers in programming, his commitment to growth serves as an inspiration to the next generation of developers. The journey of a programmer is not defined by their successes alone, but by their ability to learn, adapt, and thrive in the face of challenges.

"Mistakes are the portals of discovery." – *James Joyce*

Erich Gamma's current projects and future plans

Exploring new frontiers in programming

Erich Gamma, renowned for his pivotal contributions to software development, continues to push the boundaries of programming. His relentless pursuit of innovation has led him to explore new frontiers that challenge conventional paradigms and inspire the next generation of developers. This section delves into the current trends and emerging technologies that Gamma is passionate about, as well as the theoretical frameworks and practical challenges associated with them.

The Rise of Functional Programming

One of the most significant shifts in the programming landscape is the resurgence of functional programming (FP). Unlike traditional imperative programming, which focuses on how to perform tasks via statements, FP emphasizes the use of functions as first-class citizens. This paradigm encourages immutability and statelessness, leading to more predictable and maintainable code. Gamma has shown a keen interest in FP, recognizing its potential to simplify complex systems.

$$f(x) = x^2 + 2x + 1 \tag{17}$$

This quadratic function exemplifies how functional programming can be used to express computations in a clear and concise manner. In practical terms, languages like Haskell, Scala, and even JavaScript (with its functional features) are gaining traction among developers. Gamma advocates for the integration of FP concepts into mainstream programming practices, believing that it can lead to more robust and scalable applications.

Embracing Concurrent and Parallel Programming

As software systems become increasingly complex, the need for concurrent and parallel programming has never been more critical. Gamma emphasizes the importance of understanding concurrency models to leverage multi-core processors effectively. The challenge lies in managing shared state and ensuring thread safety, which can lead to intricate bugs if not handled properly.

Consider the following pseudo-code illustrating a simple concurrent model:

```
function process(data) {
    parallel {
        task1(data);
        task2(data);
    }
}
```

In this example, `task1` and `task2` are executed concurrently, allowing for more efficient data processing. However, Gamma warns of the pitfalls of concurrency, such as race conditions and deadlocks, which require careful design and testing. By exploring advanced concurrency patterns, such as the Actor model or using libraries like Akka, developers can create systems that are both responsive and resilient.

The Impact of Machine Learning and AI

Gamma is also captivated by the transformative potential of machine learning (ML) and artificial intelligence (AI) in programming. These technologies are not only reshaping how applications are built but also how they operate. The integration of AI into software development processes can automate mundane tasks, enhance decision-making, and even assist in debugging.

For instance, consider a scenario where an AI model predicts potential bugs in code based on historical data. The model could be trained using a dataset of previous software projects, learning to identify patterns that often lead to errors. This approach not only saves time but also improves the overall quality of the software.

$$\text{Bug Prediction} = f(\text{Code Quality Metrics, Historical Bug Data}) \quad (18)$$

Gamma believes that as AI continues to evolve, it will play a crucial role in shaping the future of programming, fostering a collaborative relationship between humans and machines.

Exploring Quantum Computing

Perhaps one of the most exciting frontiers in programming is quantum computing. Although still in its infancy, quantum computing promises to revolutionize problem-solving capabilities by leveraging the principles of quantum mechanics. Gamma is intrigued by the potential applications of quantum algorithms in fields such as cryptography, optimization, and complex simulations.

The basic unit of quantum information is the qubit, which can exist in multiple states simultaneously, unlike a classical bit, which is either 0 or 1. This property allows quantum computers to process vast amounts of data in parallel.

$$|\psi\rangle = \alpha|0\rangle + \beta|1\rangle \tag{19}$$

Here, $|\psi\rangle$ represents a quantum state, where α and β are complex numbers that describe the probability amplitudes of the qubit being in states $|0\rangle$ and $|1\rangle$. Gamma advocates for developers to familiarize themselves with quantum programming languages, such as Q# and Qiskit, to prepare for this emerging technology.

The Importance of Continuous Learning

In a rapidly evolving field like programming, continuous learning is paramount. Gamma encourages aspiring programmers to embrace lifelong learning through various means, including online courses, open-source contributions, and community engagement. By staying abreast of the latest trends and technologies, developers can remain competitive and innovative.

Moreover, Gamma emphasizes the value of collaboration and knowledge sharing within the programming community. He believes that by fostering an environment of openness and support, developers can collectively overcome challenges and drive the industry forward.

Conclusion

Erich Gamma's exploration of new frontiers in programming reflects his unwavering commitment to innovation and excellence. By embracing functional programming, concurrent systems, machine learning, and quantum computing, he is paving the way for future advancements in software development. His dedication to continuous learning and community engagement serves as an inspiration for the next generation of programmers, encouraging them to explore uncharted territories and contribute to the ever-evolving landscape of technology.

Continuing the quest for excellence

Erich Gamma's journey in the realm of software development is not merely a tale of past accomplishments; it is an ongoing pursuit of excellence that reflects his commitment to innovation and improvement. As the technology landscape evolves at an unprecedented pace, so too does Gamma's dedication to pushing the boundaries of programming practices and methodologies.

Exploring New Frontiers in Programming

Gamma's current projects are a testament to his belief in continuous learning and adaptation. He is deeply involved in several cutting-edge initiatives that explore the intersection of artificial intelligence (AI) and software engineering. The integration of AI into programming not only enhances productivity but also introduces new paradigms for problem-solving. For instance, Gamma has been a vocal advocate for leveraging machine learning algorithms to automate code generation and optimization. This approach addresses several challenges faced by developers, such as reducing the time spent on mundane coding tasks and minimizing human error.

$$\text{Code Quality} = f(\text{Automation, Testing, Review}) \qquad (20)$$

In this equation, the function f represents the relationship between code quality and the three variables: automation, testing, and review processes. By automating repetitive tasks, developers can focus on higher-level design and architecture, ultimately leading to better quality software.

Innovating Software Development Practices

In addition to his focus on AI, Gamma is also exploring innovative software development practices such as DevOps and Agile methodologies. These practices emphasize collaboration, flexibility, and rapid iteration, which are crucial in today's fast-paced development environments. Gamma's contributions in these areas have been significant, particularly in promoting the idea that development and operations should work hand in hand to create seamless workflows.

One of the key challenges in implementing DevOps is the cultural shift required within organizations. Gamma emphasizes the importance of fostering a culture of collaboration and open communication. This cultural transformation is often met with resistance, as teams may be accustomed to siloed operations. However, Gamma's advocacy for cross-functional teams has shown that embracing this change can lead to remarkable improvements in deployment frequency and software quality.

The Importance of Mentorship and Knowledge Sharing

Gamma's quest for excellence is also reflected in his commitment to mentorship and knowledge sharing within the programming community. He believes that the future of software development hinges on the ability to cultivate new talent and share best practices. By engaging with aspiring programmers through workshops, lectures, and online platforms, Gamma aims to inspire the next generation to embrace the principles of design patterns and software architecture.

For example, he has been involved in various educational initiatives that focus on teaching design patterns through practical applications. By encouraging students to apply these concepts in real-world projects, Gamma helps them understand the relevance and utility of design patterns in crafting robust software solutions.

Embracing Open Source Contributions

Another significant aspect of Gamma's current endeavors is his active participation in open source projects. He recognizes that open source software not only fosters collaboration but also accelerates innovation by allowing developers to build upon each other's work. Gamma's contributions to various open source initiatives demonstrate his belief in the power of community-driven development.

By participating in these projects, Gamma also addresses the problem of knowledge silos that often plague proprietary software development. Open source contributions facilitate transparency and collective problem-solving, enabling developers to learn from one another and advance their skills. As Gamma often states, "The best way to learn is to contribute."

Looking Ahead: The Future of Software Development

As Erich Gamma continues his journey, he remains focused on the future of software development. He is particularly interested in the implications of quantum computing and how it may revolutionize programming paradigms. While still in its infancy, quantum computing presents unique challenges and opportunities for software engineers.

Gamma envisions a future where programmers will need to rethink traditional algorithms and design patterns to accommodate the principles of quantum mechanics. This shift will require a new set of skills and a willingness to adapt to radically different computational models.

In summary, Erich Gamma's quest for excellence is characterized by his unwavering commitment to innovation, mentorship, and collaboration. As he navigates the evolving landscape of software development, he remains a beacon of inspiration for programmers worldwide, encouraging them to embrace change and strive for excellence in their own journeys. His legacy is not only defined by his past achievements but also by the impact he continues to make on the future of programming.

Controversies and Unauthorized Access

Unauthorized peek into Gamma's private life

Ethical concerns and implications

The endeavor to write an unauthorized biography, particularly one that delves into the private life of a prominent figure like Erich Gamma, raises a multitude of ethical concerns that warrant careful consideration. The intersection of biography, privacy, and the public's right to know creates a complex landscape in which ethical implications must be navigated thoughtfully.

Privacy vs. Public Interest

At the heart of the ethical debate is the tension between an individual's right to privacy and the public's interest in their life story. Erich Gamma, known for his groundbreaking contributions to software development, has a public persona that many admire. However, this does not automatically grant permission to explore his private life without consent. Privacy, as defined by *Westin's Privacy Theory*, encompasses the right of individuals to control information about themselves, which includes both personal and professional realms.

$$P = \frac{C}{I} \tag{21}$$

Where P represents privacy, C is control over personal information, and I signifies the intrusion from external sources. As such, the unauthorized biography may infringe upon Gamma's right to control his narrative, leading to potential emotional and psychological ramifications.

The Role of Consent

Consent is a fundamental ethical principle in research and writing. In the context of biographies, especially unauthorized ones, the absence of consent can lead to misrepresentation or exploitation. The ethical implications of writing about Gamma's life without his approval raise questions about the integrity of the narrative presented. As highlighted by *Bok's Model of Ethical Decision-Making*, the writer must weigh the potential harm against the benefits of disclosure.

$$E = B - H \qquad (22)$$

Where E represents the ethical justification, B is the benefits derived from the biography, and H denotes the harm inflicted on the subject. If the harm outweighs the benefits, the ethical implications of proceeding with the biography become increasingly problematic.

Potential Misrepresentation

Unauthorized biographies often risk misrepresentation, as they may rely on second-hand accounts or speculative interpretations of events. This can lead to a skewed portrayal of the subject's life, which can be damaging both personally and professionally. For instance, if the biography emphasizes controversies or unverified claims about Gamma's personal life, it could overshadow his substantial contributions to the field of software development, thereby distorting public perception.

The *Harm Principle*, articulated by philosopher John Stuart Mill, asserts that individuals should be free to act however they wish unless their actions cause harm to others. In this case, the potential harm caused by misrepresentation could not only affect Gamma's reputation but also influence the perceptions of aspiring programmers who look up to him as a role model.

The Ethical Responsibility of the Biographer

The biographer bears a significant ethical responsibility to ensure accuracy and fairness in their portrayal of the subject. This responsibility includes conducting thorough research and verifying facts to avoid the dissemination of false information. The ethical guidelines set forth by organizations such as the *Society of Professional Journalists* emphasize the importance of seeking truth and reporting it accurately.

$$A = R + V \qquad (23)$$

Where A represents accountability, R is the responsibility to the subject, and V is the value of the truth. The biographer must strive to uphold these principles, ensuring that the narrative presented is as factual and respectful as possible, even in the absence of the subject's consent.

Impact on the Subject's Legacy

Finally, the ethical implications extend to the impact of the unauthorized biography on Gamma's legacy. The portrayal of his life and work can influence how future generations perceive his contributions to the field of software engineering. A biography that focuses excessively on personal controversies may overshadow his professional achievements, creating a lasting impression that could distort his legacy.

In conclusion, the ethical concerns surrounding unauthorized biographies, particularly in the case of influential figures like Erich Gamma, highlight the delicate balance between the right to privacy and the public's right to know. By considering the implications of privacy, consent, misrepresentation, and accountability, biographers can navigate these complex ethical waters while striving to honor the legacy of their subjects.

The tangled web of privacy and fame

In the digital age, the intersection of privacy and fame presents a complex landscape, particularly for public figures like Erich Gamma. As a pivotal figure in software development, Gamma's contributions have garnered him recognition, but this fame also brings challenges regarding his personal privacy. The relationship between privacy and fame can be understood through several theoretical frameworks, including the *Social Contract Theory* and the *Public Interest Theory*.

Social Contract Theory

Social Contract Theory posits that individuals consent, either explicitly or implicitly, to surrender some of their freedoms and submit to the authority of the community in exchange for protection of their remaining rights. In Gamma's case, his fame can be seen as the result of a social contract where the public has access to his professional achievements and insights, while he, in return, sacrifices a degree of his personal privacy. This raises the question: to what extent should public figures be expected to share their personal lives?

Public Interest Theory

Public Interest Theory suggests that certain information about public figures is necessary for the public to make informed decisions. For instance, understanding Gamma's motivations, challenges, and personal experiences can provide valuable insights into his work and the evolution of design patterns. However, this theory also poses ethical dilemmas. The line between public interest and sensationalism often blurs, leading to invasive scrutiny that can impact the personal lives of individuals.

The Problems of Privacy

The challenges faced by Gamma in maintaining his privacy are multifaceted. With the rise of social media and the 24-hour news cycle, the public's appetite for information about public figures has intensified. This phenomenon can lead to:

- **Invasive Reporting:** Journalists and biographers may seek to uncover every detail of Gamma's life, often prioritizing sensational stories over respectful reporting. The unauthorized biography format can exacerbate this issue, as it may encourage speculation and conjecture rather than factual representation.

- **Mental Health Impacts:** The pressure of fame can lead to significant stress and anxiety. Public figures often grapple with the fear of misrepresentation or the loss of control over their narrative, which can affect their mental well-being.

- **Legal Repercussions:** The tension between privacy and fame can lead to legal battles over defamation, invasion of privacy, and intellectual property rights. Gamma's experiences may illustrate the broader implications of unauthorized biographies and the potential for legal action to protect personal narratives.

Examples of Privacy Invasion

Several high-profile cases in the tech industry highlight the challenges of balancing fame and privacy. For instance, the unauthorized biography of Steve Jobs, written by Walter Isaacson, provided an in-depth look at the Apple co-founder's life but also exposed Jobs to intense scrutiny regarding his personal relationships and health issues. Similarly, the public's fascination with Elon Musk's personal life often overshadows his professional achievements, raising concerns about the ethics of such coverage.

Navigating the Privacy-Fame Dichotomy

For figures like Gamma, navigating the privacy-fame dichotomy requires a careful strategy. Some potential approaches include:

- **Controlled Disclosure:** By selectively sharing personal stories and insights, Gamma can maintain a degree of control over his narrative. This approach allows him to engage with the public while safeguarding aspects of his private life.

- **Advocacy for Privacy Rights:** Public figures can advocate for stronger privacy protections in the media, emphasizing the importance of ethical journalism and responsible reporting.

- **Engagement with the Community:** Building a supportive community can help public figures navigate the challenges of fame. By fostering relationships with fans and colleagues, Gamma can create a buffer against negative scrutiny.

In conclusion, the tangled web of privacy and fame presents significant challenges for Erich Gamma and other public figures in the tech industry. Understanding the theoretical frameworks that underpin this relationship is crucial for navigating the complexities of public life while striving to maintain personal integrity and privacy. As the boundaries between public and private continue to blur, the dialogue surrounding the rights of public figures will remain a critical conversation in our society.

Challenges faced in writing an unauthorized biography

Gathering reliable information

In the realm of unauthorized biographies, the quest for reliable information can be both a challenging and intricate endeavor. The very essence of biographical writing hinges on the accuracy and authenticity of the details presented, particularly when the subject has not consented to the portrayal of their life. This section explores the theoretical foundations, practical problems, and illustrative examples of gathering reliable information about Erich Gamma, a prominent figure in the software development community.

Theoretical Foundations

The process of gathering reliable information is rooted in the principles of research methodology, which emphasizes the importance of validity, reliability, and credibility. Validity refers to the extent to which the information accurately reflects the subject's life and contributions, while reliability pertains to the consistency of the information across different sources. Credibility, on the other hand, assesses the trustworthiness of the sources from which the information is derived.

$$\text{Reliability} = \frac{\text{Number of consistent sources}}{\text{Total number of sources}} \times 100 \qquad (24)$$

In the context of unauthorized biographies, it is imperative to utilize a diverse array of sources to ensure a well-rounded perspective. These sources can include:

- **Interviews:** Conversations with colleagues, friends, and family members who have insights into Gamma's life and work.

- **Published Works:** Academic papers, articles, and books authored by or about Gamma that provide context and analysis of his contributions.

- **Media Coverage:** News articles, interviews, and documentaries that discuss Gamma's impact on the software industry.

- **Social Media:** Online platforms where Gamma or others may have shared personal anecdotes or reflections about his career.

Practical Problems

Despite the array of potential sources, several practical problems can arise during the information-gathering process:

- **Bias and Subjectivity:** Personal accounts may be colored by the interviewee's biases, leading to skewed representations of Gamma's character or achievements. For instance, a close colleague may emphasize Gamma's collaborative spirit, while a competitor might focus on his competitive nature.

- **Inaccessibility of Sources:** Some individuals who could provide valuable insights may be unwilling or unavailable to speak. This can limit the depth of understanding regarding Gamma's personal and professional life.

+ **Conflicting Accounts:** Different sources may present conflicting narratives about the same event or period in Gamma's life. For example, one source might describe a pivotal meeting that led to the formation of the "Gang of Four," while another might provide a completely different version of the event.

+ **Legal and Ethical Considerations:** Unauthorized biographies often tread a fine line between public interest and personal privacy. The risk of legal repercussions can deter potential sources from sharing sensitive information.

Illustrative Examples

To illustrate the complexities of gathering reliable information, consider the following examples from the life of Erich Gamma:

+ **Interviews with Peers:** Engaging with Gamma's peers in the software development community can yield valuable insights. However, discrepancies in their recollections may arise. For instance, while one colleague might recall Gamma's innovative approach to problem-solving, another may highlight his meticulous attention to detail. These differing perspectives necessitate careful analysis and cross-referencing to construct an accurate portrayal.

+ **Published Works:** Gamma's contributions to design patterns are well-documented in academic literature. However, the interpretation of his work can vary. Some authors may emphasize the theoretical aspects of design patterns, while others focus on practical applications. It is crucial to synthesize these viewpoints to provide a comprehensive understanding of Gamma's influence.

+ **Media Coverage:** Articles from technology magazines may celebrate Gamma's achievements but can also perpetuate myths or exaggerations. For example, a sensationalized account of his role in the software revolution could overshadow the collaborative nature of his work, necessitating a balanced approach in the biography.

In conclusion, gathering reliable information for an unauthorized biography of Erich Gamma involves navigating a complex landscape of sources, biases, and ethical considerations. By employing rigorous research methodologies and critically evaluating the information obtained, biographers can strive to present an accurate and nuanced portrayal of this influential programmer's life and legacy.

The risk of legal repercussions

When embarking on the journey of writing an unauthorized biography, one must tread carefully through the intricate web of legal implications that may arise. The act of delving into the personal life of a public figure, such as Erich Gamma, can evoke a myriad of legal challenges, primarily revolving around issues of privacy, defamation, and intellectual property.

Privacy Concerns

The right to privacy is a fundamental legal principle that protects individuals from unwarranted intrusion into their personal lives. In many jurisdictions, public figures, including programmers and tech leaders, have a reduced expectation of privacy due to their public status. However, this does not grant biographers carte blanche to disclose every detail of their lives.

$$\text{Expectation of Privacy} = f(\text{Public Status, Nature of Information}) \qquad (25)$$

For instance, while Gamma's professional achievements may be fair game for discussion, personal matters such as family dynamics or private relationships could lead to legal action if disclosed without consent. Courts often consider the context and relevance of the information in question, weighing public interest against the individual's right to privacy.

Defamation Risks

Defamation poses another significant risk in unauthorized biographies. Defamation occurs when false statements are presented as facts that damage an individual's reputation. In the context of Gamma's biography, if any claims regarding his character or professional conduct are made without substantial evidence, the author could face legal repercussions.

$$\text{Defamation} = \text{False Statement} + \text{Publication} + \text{Harm} \qquad (26)$$

To mitigate this risk, it is essential to ensure that all statements are well-researched and backed by credible sources. Moreover, including a disclaimer that clarifies the nature of the content as opinion rather than fact may provide some legal protection, although it does not guarantee immunity from lawsuits.

Intellectual Property Issues

Another layer of complexity arises from intellectual property rights. Unauthorized biographies may inadvertently infringe on copyrights, especially if they include unpublished works, photographs, or proprietary information without permission. For example, if Gamma's unpublished code or design documents are referenced without proper authorization, it could lead to a copyright infringement claim.

$$\text{Infringement Risk} = f(\text{Use of Work, Permission Status}) \qquad (27)$$

To navigate this terrain, biographers should seek to obtain permissions whenever possible and ensure that any use of copyrighted material falls under the fair use doctrine. Fair use typically allows for limited use of copyrighted material for purposes such as criticism, comment, or scholarship, but its application can be subjective and context-dependent.

Case Studies and Precedents

Several high-profile unauthorized biographies have faced legal challenges, providing valuable lessons for aspiring authors. For instance, the biography of a famous musician faced a lawsuit over privacy invasion when it disclosed intimate details about the musician's family life. The court ruled in favor of the musician, emphasizing the importance of consent and privacy.

In another notable case, a biography of a public figure was met with defamation claims after it included allegations of misconduct without sufficient evidence. The resulting legal battle highlighted the necessity for thorough fact-checking and the potential financial repercussions of a defamation suit.

Conclusion

In conclusion, while the endeavor to write an unauthorized biography can be an exciting and rewarding venture, it is fraught with legal risks that must be carefully navigated. Authors must remain vigilant about privacy rights, defamation laws, and intellectual property issues to mitigate the potential for legal repercussions. Engaging with legal professionals during the writing process can provide invaluable guidance and help ensure that the biography remains both compelling and legally sound.

Ultimately, the goal should be to honor the subject's legacy while respecting their rights, striking a balance between storytelling and ethical responsibility.

The impact of unauthorized access to Gamma's life

A new perspective on a famous programmer's journey

The life of Erich Gamma, a name synonymous with the revolution in software design, is often viewed through a narrow lens of his professional achievements. However, an unauthorized biography offers a unique opportunity to delve deeper into the complexities of his journey, revealing not just the milestones but also the struggles, aspirations, and the human side of a programming icon.

To fully appreciate Gamma's impact, it is essential to understand the context of his work within the broader landscape of software engineering. The emergence of design patterns, particularly the seminal work produced by the "Gang of Four," did not occur in a vacuum. It was the culmination of years of theoretical development and practical experimentation. The journey to this pivotal moment was fraught with challenges, skepticism, and an evolving understanding of what constitutes effective software architecture.

One key aspect that often gets overshadowed is the theoretical underpinnings of design patterns. The concept of design patterns in software engineering can be traced back to Christopher Alexander's work in architecture, where he proposed that certain solutions recur in various contexts. This idea was adapted by Gamma and his colleagues to suit the needs of software development, leading to the formulation of a catalog of common solutions to recurring design problems. The significance of this theoretical foundation cannot be overstated; it provided a framework that allowed programmers to communicate more effectively and to build upon each other's work.

In Gamma's case, the journey was not merely about creating a reference book; it was about fostering a paradigm shift in how software development was approached. His collaborative efforts with industry leaders were marked by rigorous debates and discussions, which were instrumental in refining the concepts that would eventually be documented in "Design Patterns: Elements of Reusable Object-Oriented Software." This book not only served as a guide but also challenged existing methodologies, pushing the boundaries of traditional programming practices.

However, the path to recognition was not without its hurdles. The initial reception of design patterns was met with skepticism from some quarters of the software community. Critics questioned the necessity of such abstractions, arguing that they added unnecessary complexity to software design. This skepticism reflects a broader tension within the programming community regarding the balance between innovation and practicality. Gamma's perseverance in the face of such challenges speaks volumes about his commitment to advancing the field.

Moreover, the unauthorized nature of this biography allows for an exploration of the personal sacrifices Gamma made during his ascent to prominence. The pressure to produce groundbreaking work often comes at the cost of personal relationships and mental well-being. Balancing the demands of fame with the desire for a fulfilling personal life is a theme that resonates with many who have achieved success in their respective fields. Gamma's journey illustrates this struggle, revealing how the pursuit of excellence can sometimes lead to isolation and self-doubt.

An example of this can be seen in the way Gamma approached his work on the design patterns. The iterative process of refining these concepts involved countless hours of collaboration, research, and revision. The emotional toll of striving for perfection in a highly competitive environment cannot be understated.   In interviews, Gamma has reflected on the late nights spent debating the nuances of design patterns with his colleagues, often at the expense of time spent with family and friends.

Furthermore, the unauthorized biography sheds light on the ethical dilemmas faced by Gamma and his peers. The question of credit and recognition is a recurring theme in collaborative projects. While the "Gang of Four" is celebrated for their contributions, the complexities of authorship in a field that thrives on collaboration are often murky. Gamma's reflections on these issues provide a nuanced perspective on the nature of success in the tech industry, where the lines between individual and collective achievement can blur.

In conclusion, the unauthorized exploration of Erich Gamma's journey offers a fresh lens through which to view his contributions to software engineering. It challenges the reader to consider not just the accolades and achievements but also the personal struggles, ethical dilemmas, and theoretical foundations that shaped his work.   By embracing this multifaceted perspective, we can gain a deeper appreciation for the legacy of a programmer who not only changed the industry but also navigated the complexities of fame, collaboration, and innovation. This new perspective serves as a reminder that behind every great achievement lies a story of perseverance, passion, and the relentless pursuit of knowledge.

Ethical debates surrounding unauthorized biographies

The emergence of unauthorized biographies has sparked significant ethical debates within literary and academic circles. These discussions often revolve around the concepts of privacy, consent, and the moral responsibilities of biographers. Unauthorized biographies, by their nature, delve into the lives of individuals without their explicit permission, raising questions about the ethical implications of such actions.

One of the primary ethical concerns is the issue of **privacy**. Individuals, regardless of their public status, possess an inherent right to privacy. This principle is grounded in the belief that everyone should have control over their personal narrative. For instance, consider the case of a celebrity whose life is chronicled without their consent. The biographer may uncover sensitive information, leading to potential emotional distress or reputational harm for the subject. This situation exemplifies the conflict between the public's right to know and the individual's right to privacy.

Furthermore, the concept of **informed consent** plays a crucial role in these debates. In traditional biographical practices, obtaining consent from the subject or their estate is considered a standard ethical guideline. However, unauthorized biographies often bypass this step, raising questions about the integrity of the biographical process. Critics argue that without consent, the biographer may misrepresent the subject's life or intentions, leading to a distorted portrayal. For example, the unauthorized biography of a public figure may focus disproportionately on scandalous events, overshadowing their professional achievements or personal struggles.

Additionally, the motivations behind writing unauthorized biographies can also be scrutinized. Biographers may be driven by a desire for financial gain or sensationalism rather than a genuine interest in the subject's life. This raises the question of **moral responsibility**. A biographer's obligation should extend beyond mere storytelling; they should strive to present a balanced and fair representation of their subject. When financial incentives overshadow ethical considerations, the integrity of the biography is compromised.

Another significant aspect of this debate is the impact of unauthorized biographies on the subject's **legacy**. An unauthorized biography can shape public perception and influence how future generations view an individual. For instance, if a biography presents a one-dimensional view of a complex figure, it risks overshadowing their contributions and achievements. This can lead to a skewed understanding of their legacy, which may persist long after the biography is published.

Moreover, the ethical implications of unauthorized biographies are compounded by the advent of digital media. In the age of the internet, information can be disseminated rapidly, making it challenging to control narratives. Unauthorized biographies can gain traction quickly, leading to widespread misconceptions. This highlights the need for a more nuanced approach to biographical writing, emphasizing the importance of accuracy and fairness.

In conclusion, the ethical debates surrounding unauthorized biographies reflect a complex interplay of privacy, consent, moral responsibility, and legacy. As biographers navigate these challenges, they must consider the implications of their work on the individuals they portray. Striking a balance between the public's curiosity and the subject's rights is essential to uphold the integrity of biographical literature. The discussions surrounding these ethical dilemmas are crucial in shaping the future of biography as a genre, ensuring that it remains a respectful and meaningful exploration of human lives.

Conclusion

The lasting impact of Erich Gamma's contributions

Design patterns as a cornerstone of software engineering

In the realm of software engineering, design patterns serve as the foundational building blocks that enable developers to create robust, maintainable, and scalable software systems. They encapsulate best practices and provide standardized solutions to common problems encountered during software development. This section delves into the significance of design patterns, illustrating how they have become indispensable in the craft of software engineering.

The Significance of Design Patterns

Design patterns are not merely theoretical constructs; they represent the collective wisdom of experienced software engineers who have faced similar challenges. By documenting these solutions, design patterns facilitate communication among developers, allowing them to share insights and foster collaboration. Each design pattern provides a template for solving a specific problem, making it easier for programmers to understand and implement solutions.

One of the core reasons design patterns are essential in software engineering is their ability to promote code reusability. When developers implement a design pattern, they can leverage proven solutions rather than reinventing the wheel. This not only accelerates the development process but also enhances the quality of the software, as the patterns have been tested and refined over time.

Common Problems Addressed by Design Patterns

Design patterns address a variety of common problems that arise in software development. Here, we explore a few key categories of design patterns and the issues they help solve:

+ **Creational Patterns:** These patterns deal with object creation mechanisms, aiming to create objects in a manner suitable to the situation. For instance, the *Singleton* pattern ensures that a class has only one instance and provides a global point of access to it. This is particularly useful in scenarios such as logging, where a single log file should be managed by one instance.

+ **Structural Patterns:** These patterns focus on the composition of classes and objects to form larger structures. The *Adapter* pattern, for example, allows incompatible interfaces to work together. This is commonly used when integrating legacy systems with new applications, ensuring that different systems can communicate without extensive modifications.

+ **Behavioral Patterns:** These patterns deal with object interaction and responsibility. The *Observer* pattern is a prime example, allowing an object to notify other objects about changes in its state. This pattern is widely used in event-driven systems, such as user interfaces, where multiple components need to react to user actions.

Real-World Examples of Design Patterns

To illustrate the practical application of design patterns, consider the following examples:

Example 1: Singleton Pattern   In a web application that manages user sessions, the Singleton pattern can be employed to ensure that only one instance of the session manager exists throughout the application. This guarantees that all parts of the application refer to the same session data, preventing inconsistencies and ensuring that user information is accurately maintained.

Example 2: Adapter Pattern   When integrating a payment gateway into an e-commerce platform, the Adapter pattern can be utilized to bridge the gap between the existing system and the payment provider's API. By creating an adapter that translates the e-commerce platform's requests into a format understood by the payment gateway, developers can seamlessly add new payment options without altering the core application logic.

Example 3: Observer Pattern   In a stock market application, the Observer pattern can be implemented to notify multiple clients about stock price changes. When a stock's price updates, the subject (stock) notifies all registered observers (clients), allowing them to react accordingly, such as updating their dashboards or triggering alerts.

The Enduring Relevance of Design Patterns

The relevance of design patterns extends beyond their initial implementation. As software systems evolve, the principles encapsulated in design patterns continue to provide guidance in maintaining and scaling applications. They serve as a common language for developers, bridging gaps between teams and fostering a culture of collaboration.

Moreover, design patterns are not static; they evolve alongside technology. New patterns emerge as developers encounter novel challenges, while existing patterns are refined to adapt to modern development practices, such as agile methodologies and microservices architecture.

In conclusion, design patterns are indeed the cornerstone of software engineering. They provide a structured approach to solving problems, enhance code quality, and facilitate communication among developers. As the software landscape continues to evolve, the principles and practices encapsulated in design patterns will remain vital in shaping the future of software development.

Inspiring the next generation of programmers

The legacy of Erich Gamma extends far beyond the pages of design patterns; it resonates deeply within the hearts and minds of aspiring programmers around the globe. His contributions have not only shaped the field of software engineering but have also inspired countless individuals to pursue their passions in coding and technology. In this section, we explore how Gamma's work serves as a beacon of motivation for the next generation of programmers.

The Power of Design Patterns

At the core of Gamma's influence lies the concept of design patterns, which serve as standardized solutions to common problems in software design. By demystifying complex programming challenges, Gamma has equipped budding programmers with the tools they need to think critically and creatively.

For instance, consider the **Singleton Pattern**, which restricts a class to a single instance and provides a global point of access to it. This pattern addresses the problem of resource management, ensuring that a particular resource is not duplicated unnecessarily. The implementation can be illustrated as follows:

```
class Singleton {
private:
    static Singleton* instance;
    Singleton() {}
public:
    static Singleton* getInstance() {
        if (!instance) {
            instance = new Singleton();
        }
        return\index{return} instance\index{instance};
    }
};
```

By introducing such patterns in educational curricula, instructors can help students understand the importance of reusability and maintainability in code, fostering a mindset geared toward solving problems efficiently.

Mentorship and Community Engagement

Gamma's journey also highlights the significance of mentorship in nurturing future talent. He has been actively involved in various programming communities, sharing his knowledge and experiences through talks, workshops, and open-source contributions. This engagement not only helps demystify advanced concepts but also encourages a collaborative spirit among programmers.

For example, initiatives like **Hackathons** have become platforms where experienced developers mentor novices, guiding them through real-world projects. Such environments foster innovation, teamwork, and a sense of belonging, all of which are crucial for young programmers.

Emphasizing Problem-Solving Skills

One of the most valuable lessons from Gamma's work is the emphasis on problem-solving. By encouraging aspiring programmers to tackle challenges head-on, he instills a mindset that is essential for success in the tech industry.

Consider the **Observer Pattern**, which allows an object to notify other objects about changes in its state. This pattern exemplifies how understanding relationships between components can lead to more effective solutions. The implementation can be summarized as follows:

```cpp
class Subject {
private:
    std::list<Observer*> observers;
public:
    void attach(Observer* observer) {
        observers.push_back(observer);
    }
    void notify() {
        for (Observer* observer : observers) {
            observer->update();
        }
    }
};
```

In teaching this pattern, educators can challenge students to think critically about how changes in one part of a system can impact others, thereby honing their analytical skills.

Encouraging Lifelong Learning

Gamma's journey underscores the importance of lifelong learning in the ever-evolving field of programming. He exemplifies the notion that curiosity and adaptability are crucial traits for success. By sharing his own experiences of continuous learning—whether through formal education, self-study, or professional development—Gamma inspires young programmers to embrace a similar path.

This commitment to learning can be fostered through various means:

+ **Online Courses:** Platforms like Coursera and Udacity provide access to high-quality programming courses, allowing students to learn at their own pace.

+ **Open Source Contributions:** Engaging with open-source projects not only enhances coding skills but also builds a sense of community and collaboration.

+ **Networking Events:** Conferences and meetups offer opportunities to connect with industry leaders, gaining insights and inspiration from their experiences.

Conclusion

In conclusion, Erich Gamma's contributions to software development are a source of inspiration for the next generation of programmers. By emphasizing the significance of design patterns, mentorship, problem-solving, and lifelong learning, he has created a legacy that encourages young minds to explore the vast possibilities within the tech landscape. As they embark on their own journeys, they carry with them the torch lit by pioneers like Gamma, illuminating the path for future innovators in the world of programming.

A tribute to Erich Gamma's untold journey

Unveiling the unknown aspects of a famous programmer's life

In the world of software engineering, the spotlight often shines brightly on the achievements of its luminaries, but what about the shadows that linger in the corners of their lives? The biography of Erich Gamma, co-author of the seminal work *Design Patterns: Elements of Reusable Object-Oriented Software*, offers a tantalizing glimpse into the unknown aspects of a celebrated programmer's journey. This section aims to peel back the layers of Gamma's life, revealing the intricacies that shaped him not just as a programmer, but as a person.

The Human Side of Genius

Behind every great programmer lies a human story, often filled with trials, tribulations, and triumphs. Erich Gamma's journey is no exception. Born in Zurich, Switzerland, he was not just a prodigy; he was a son, a friend, and a member of a community. His upbringing in a family that valued education and hard work laid the foundation for his future success. However, the pressure to excel can be a double-edged sword. The expectations of family and society can lead to a sense of isolation, even for those who appear to have it all.

Gamma's early encounters with computers ignited a passion that would consume him. Yet, this passion came with its own set of challenges. The late 1970s and early 1980s were a time of rapid technological advancement, and as a young programmer, Gamma faced the daunting task of keeping pace with an ever-evolving landscape. The thrill of coding was often tempered by the fear of obsolescence. This paradox is not uncommon among tech professionals, where the relentless march of progress can overshadow personal achievements.

Mentorship and Influence

Mentorship plays a crucial role in shaping the trajectories of aspiring programmers. For Gamma, key figures in his academic and professional life provided guidance and inspiration. These mentors were not merely instructors; they were catalysts for his growth, pushing him to explore the depths of programming beyond the classroom. The relationship between mentor and mentee is often complex, characterized by admiration, rivalry, and sometimes, a quest for validation.

Consider the role of the "Gang of Four," the collective that included Gamma and his colleagues. Their collaboration on design patterns was not just a professional endeavor; it was a crucible of ideas, where differing perspectives clashed and coalesced into something greater. The friction of collaboration can lead to breakthroughs, but it can also reveal the vulnerabilities of those involved. The dynamics within the group, including moments of conflict and consensus, provide a rich tapestry for understanding Gamma's contributions and the collaborative spirit that underpinned the development of design patterns.

The Burden of Recognition

As Gamma's work gained prominence, he was thrust into the limelight, a position that came with its own set of challenges. The burden of recognition can weigh heavily on individuals, leading to a constant struggle for balance between personal fulfillment and public expectation. In the software community, where contributions are often scrutinized and debated, Gamma's role in the creation of design patterns has sparked discussions about authorship and credit.

The controversies surrounding the attribution of ideas can be profound. While the *Gang of Four* collectively created a monumental work, individual contributions can become obscured in the narrative of success. Gamma's experience highlights a broader issue in the tech industry: the tension between collaboration and individual recognition. As programmers, we often grapple with the desire for acknowledgment while simultaneously valuing the collaborative nature of our work.

Personal Life and Public Persona

The dichotomy between personal life and public persona is another aspect that often remains hidden in the biographies of famous programmers. Gamma's journey illustrates the delicate balance he navigated between his professional ambitions and his personal relationships. The demands of fame can strain familial bonds and friendships, leading to a sense of disconnection from the very people who support us.

In interviews, Gamma has reflected on the sacrifices made in pursuit of excellence. The late nights spent coding and the relentless pursuit of perfection can come at a cost. The emotional toll of success, coupled with the pressure to maintain a public image, often leaves little room for vulnerability. Understanding the emotional landscape of a programmer like Gamma provides valuable insights into the human experience behind the code.

Lessons from the Shadows

Unveiling the unknown aspects of Erich Gamma's life reveals important lessons for aspiring programmers and industry veterans alike. First, it underscores the importance of mentorship and collaboration. The tech industry thrives on shared knowledge, and the relationships we build can shape our careers in profound ways.

Secondly, it highlights the need for balance. Success is not solely defined by professional achievements; personal fulfillment and relationships are equally vital. As we navigate our careers, it is essential to remember that the journey is as important as the destination.

Finally, the exploration of Gamma's life prompts us to consider the ethical implications of fame and recognition in the tech industry. As we celebrate the contributions of programming pioneers, we must also acknowledge the complexities of their journeys, including the challenges they faced and the sacrifices they made.

In conclusion, the untold aspects of Erich Gamma's life offer a richer understanding of his legacy. By delving into the shadows of his journey, we gain a more nuanced perspective on the man behind the code, reminding us that behind every line of programming, there lies a story worth telling.

Acknowledging the legacy of a programming pioneer

The journey of Erich Gamma is not merely a tale of personal achievement; it is a profound narrative that intertwines with the evolution of software engineering itself. As we delve into the legacy left by this programming pioneer, it is essential to recognize how his contributions have shaped the landscape of software development and influenced generations of programmers.

The Foundations of Software Engineering

At the heart of Gamma's legacy lies the introduction of design patterns, a concept that revolutionized the way software is architected. Design patterns provide standardized solutions to common problems encountered in software design, facilitating clearer communication among developers and enhancing code maintainability. This concept is encapsulated in the famous definition by Christopher Alexander, who stated that a pattern is a solution to a recurring problem in a given context. Gamma, along with his colleagues, distilled this idea into a practical framework for software development, leading to the publication of the seminal book, *Design Patterns: Elements of Reusable Object-Oriented Software*.

The impact of this work can be understood through the following equation that represents the relationship between software quality and design patterns:

$$Q = f(P, R, C) \tag{28}$$

Where:

- Q represents the overall quality of the software.

- P denotes the use of design patterns.

- R is the level of code reusability.

- C signifies the clarity of the codebase.

This equation illustrates that as the use of design patterns (P) increases, so too does the quality (Q) of the software, driven by enhanced reusability (R) and clarity (C).

Real-World Applications

The principles laid out by Gamma have been adopted across various domains, from web development to embedded systems. For instance, consider the Singleton pattern, which ensures that a class has only one instance and provides a global point of access to it. This pattern has been widely utilized in database connection pooling, where multiple requests need to access a single database instance efficiently.

To illustrate, consider the following pseudocode for a Singleton pattern implementation:

```
class DatabaseConnection {
    private static\index{static} instance\index{instance}: Datab

    private constructor() {
        // Initialize connection
    }
```

```
public static getInstance(): DatabaseConnection {
    if (instance == null) {
        instance = new DatabaseConnection();
    }
    return\index{return} instance\index{instance};
}
}
```

This implementation ensures that the 'DatabaseConnection' class can only be instantiated once, thereby preventing resource exhaustion and ensuring consistent access to the database.

Inspiring Future Generations

Gamma's legacy extends beyond design patterns; it encompasses his role as a mentor and leader in the programming community. His commitment to sharing knowledge and fostering innovation has inspired countless programmers to pursue excellence in their craft. Through his work at IBM and various conferences, Gamma has emphasized the importance of collaboration and continuous learning in software development.

The influence of Gamma can be seen in the rise of communities dedicated to software craftsmanship, where the focus is on writing clean, efficient, and maintainable code. This movement echoes Gamma's principles, encouraging developers to embrace best practices and prioritize quality over quantity.

Conclusion

In acknowledging the legacy of Erich Gamma, we must recognize the profound impact he has had on the field of software engineering. His pioneering work on design patterns not only provided solutions to complex design challenges but also fostered a culture of collaboration and knowledge sharing among developers. As we move forward in an ever-evolving technological landscape, Gamma's contributions will continue to serve as a cornerstone for aspiring programmers, guiding them in their quest for excellence in software development.

The journey of Erich Gamma is a testament to the power of innovation, collaboration, and the relentless pursuit of knowledge. His legacy is not just a chapter in the history of programming; it is a living, breathing influence that will inspire future generations to push the boundaries of what is possible in the world of software engineering.

Acknowledgments and Sources

Sources consulted for this biography

Expressing gratitude towards those who contributed to the book's creation

The importance of research and accuracy in biographical works

Appendix: Selected Design Patterns

Creational Patterns

Factory Method

The Factory Method is a creational design pattern that provides an interface for creating objects in a superclass, but allows subclasses to alter the type of objects that will be created. This pattern is particularly useful when the exact types of objects to be created are not known until runtime, enabling greater flexibility and scalability in software development.

Theory

The Factory Method encapsulates the instantiation logic, allowing the system to be more decoupled and easier to extend. Instead of calling a constructor directly, the client code calls a factory method that returns an instance of a product. This decoupling allows for the introduction of new products without changing the existing client code.

$$\text{Product} = \text{Factory Method} \rightarrow \text{Concrete Product} \qquad (29)$$

In this equation, the Factory Method acts as an intermediary that returns a Concrete Product based on the implementation in the subclass.

Structure

The Factory Method pattern typically involves the following components:

- **Product:** Defines the interface of objects that the factory method creates.

117

- **ConcreteProduct**: Implements the Product interface.

- **Creator**: Declares the factory method, which returns a Product object. The Creator may also provide some default implementation of the factory method.

- **ConcreteCreator**: Overrides the factory method to return an instance of a ConcreteProduct.

Problems Addressed

The Factory Method pattern addresses several common problems in software design:

- **Tight Coupling**: By using the Factory Method, client code is decoupled from the concrete classes it instantiates. This reduces the impact of changes in the product classes.

- **Code Duplication**: The pattern promotes code reuse by centralizing the instantiation logic in the factory method.

- **Scalability**: New products can be added with minimal changes to the existing codebase, allowing the system to grow without significant refactoring.

Example

Consider a scenario where we need to create different types of vehicles. Instead of directly instantiating the vehicles, we can use the Factory Method.

```
class Vehicle {
    public function drive() {
        // Driving logic
    }
}

class Car extends Vehicle {
    public function drive() {
        // Car-specific driving logic
    }
}

class Truck extends Vehicle {
    public function drive() {
```

```
        // Truck-specific driving logic
    }
}

abstract class VehicleFactory {
    abstract public function createVehicle(): Vehicle;
}

class CarFactory extends VehicleFactory {
    public function createVehicle(): Vehicle {
        return new Car();
    }
}

class TruckFactory extends VehicleFactory {
    public function createVehicle(): Vehicle {
        return new Truck();
    }
}
```

In this example, the `VehicleFactory` is an abstract class that declares the factory method `createVehicle()`. The `CarFactory` and `TruckFactory` classes implement this method to return instances of `Car` and `Truck`, respectively.

Conclusion

The Factory Method pattern is a powerful tool in a programmer's toolkit, offering a structured approach to object creation that promotes loose coupling, scalability, and maintainability. By leveraging this pattern, developers can create systems that are not only robust but also adaptable to changing requirements.

In summary, the Factory Method pattern exemplifies the principles of object-oriented design, providing a clear separation between the creation of objects and their usage, leading to cleaner, more maintainable code.

Abstract Factory

The Abstract Factory pattern is a creational design pattern that provides an interface for creating families of related or dependent objects without specifying their concrete classes. This pattern is particularly useful when a system needs to be independent of how its objects are created, composed, and represented. It allows for the creation of objects that share a common theme or functionality, ensuring that they are compatible with each other.

Theory

The Abstract Factory pattern works by defining an interface for creating objects, which is implemented by concrete factories. Each concrete factory corresponds to a specific family of products. The client code interacts with the abstract factory and uses it to create products, without needing to know the details of the concrete implementations.

$$AbstractFactory \rightarrow createProductA() \quad and \quad createProductB() \qquad (30)$$

The key components of the Abstract Factory pattern include:

+ **AbstractFactory**: An interface declaring the creation methods for different types of products.

+ **ConcreteFactory**: Implements the AbstractFactory interface to create concrete products.

+ **AbstractProduct**: An interface for the products created by the factory.

+ **ConcreteProduct**: Implements the AbstractProduct interface.

+ **Client**: Uses the AbstractFactory and AbstractProduct interfaces to work with the created products.

Problems Addressed

The Abstract Factory pattern addresses several problems in software design:

+ **Coupling**: It reduces coupling between the client code and the concrete classes. By relying on interfaces, the client can work with any family of products without being tied to specific implementations.

+ **Interchangeability**: It allows for easy interchangeability of product families. If a new family of products is introduced, the client code can remain unchanged, provided that the new family adheres to the same interfaces.

+ **Consistency:** It ensures that products created by the same factory are compatible. This is crucial in systems where products must work together seamlessly.

Example

To illustrate the Abstract Factory pattern, consider a scenario where we are developing a graphical user interface (GUI) toolkit that can create different themes for buttons and text fields. We can define an abstract factory for creating these UI components.

```
interface GUIFactory {
    Button createButton();
    TextField createTextField();
}
```

Next, we implement concrete factories for different themes:

```
class WinFactory implements GUIFactory {
    public Button createButton() {
        return new WinButton();
    }
    public TextField createTextField() {
        return new WinTextField();
    }
}

class MacFactory implements GUIFactory {
    public Button createButton() {
        return new MacButton();
    }
    public TextField createTextField() {
        return new MacTextField();
    }
}
```

The client code can then use the factory to create UI components without knowing the specifics of the implementations:

```
GUIFactory factory\index{factory};
if (isWindows) {
    factory = new WinFactory();
} else {
    factory = new MacFactory();
}

Button button = factory.createButton();
TextField textField = factory.createTextField();
```

In this example, the client code can easily switch between different themes by changing the factory instance, demonstrating the flexibility and scalability of the Abstract Factory pattern.

Conclusion

The Abstract Factory pattern is a powerful tool in the software developer's toolkit, allowing for the creation of families of related objects while promoting loose coupling and ensuring compatibility. By leveraging this pattern, developers can build more flexible and maintainable systems that can adapt to changing requirements and new product families with minimal disruption.

$$\text{Abstract Factory} \rightarrow \text{Concrete Factory} \rightarrow \text{Concrete Product} \qquad (31)$$

Singleton

The Singleton design pattern is a creational pattern that restricts the instantiation of a class to a single instance and provides a global point of access to that instance. This pattern is particularly useful when exactly one object is needed to coordinate actions across the system.

Theory

The core idea behind the Singleton pattern is to ensure that a class has only one instance and to provide a global access point to that instance. This is achieved by:

- Making the constructor private or protected to prevent instantiation from outside the class.

- Creating a static method that acts as a constructor. This method calls the constructor to create the instance if it does not already exist.

* Storing the instance in a static variable within the class.

The Singleton pattern is often used in scenarios where a single instance of a class is required to control access to resources such as database connections or configuration settings.

Problems Addressed

The Singleton pattern addresses several common problems in software design:

* **Global State Management:** It provides a controlled way to manage global state across an application without resorting to global variables.

* **Resource Management:** It ensures that resource-intensive objects are created only once, thereby conserving system resources.

* **Consistency:** By limiting instantiation to a single object, the pattern helps maintain consistency in the application's state.

However, the Singleton pattern can introduce certain challenges:

* **Testing Difficulties:** Singletons can make unit testing more challenging because they introduce global state, which can lead to hidden dependencies between tests.

* **Concurrency Issues:** In multi-threaded applications, care must be taken to ensure that the Singleton instance is created in a thread-safe manner.

Implementation Example

Below is a simple implementation of the Singleton pattern in Python:

```
class\index{class} Singleton\index{Singleton}:
    _instance = None

    def __new__(cls):
        if cls._instance is None:
            cls._instance = super(Singleton, cls).__new__(cls)
        return cls._instance

\# Usage
```

```
singleton1 = Singleton()
singleton2 = Singleton()

assert singleton1 is singleton2   \# This will be True
```

In this example, the '__new__' method is overridden to control the instantiation process. The first time a 'Singleton' object is created, the instance is stored in the class variable '_instance'. Subsequent calls to create a new 'Singleton' object will return the existing instance.

Thread-Safe Singleton

In multi-threaded environments, it is crucial to ensure that the Singleton instance is created in a thread-safe manner. One way to achieve this is by using a locking mechanism:

```
import\index{import} threading\index{threading}

class\index{class} ThreadSafeSingleton:
    _instance = None
    _lock = threading.Lock()

    def __new__(cls):
        with cls._lock:
            if cls._instance is None:
                cls._instance = super(ThreadSafeSingleton, cls).__
        return cls._instance

\# Usage
singleton1 = ThreadSafeSingleton()
singleton2 = ThreadSafeSingleton()

assert singleton1 is singleton2   \# This will be True
```

In this implementation, a lock is used to ensure that only one thread can create the instance at a time, thus preventing multiple instances from being created in a concurrent environment.

Conclusion

The Singleton design pattern is a powerful tool in a programmer's arsenal, especially when managing shared resources or maintaining global state. However, it is essential to apply it judiciously, considering the potential drawbacks and ensuring that it does not hinder the testability and maintainability of the code.

In summary, the Singleton pattern provides a structured approach to managing single instances in software design, ensuring consistency and resource efficiency while also presenting challenges that require careful consideration during implementation.

Builder

The Builder pattern is a creational design pattern that provides a flexible solution for constructing complex objects. Unlike other creational patterns, which focus on the construction process, the Builder pattern allows for the step-by-step creation of a product, enabling the construction of different representations of the same type of object. This pattern is particularly useful when an object requires numerous parameters to be set, or when the construction process involves multiple steps that can vary.

Theory

The Builder pattern separates the construction of a complex object from its representation, allowing the same construction process to create different representations. It involves a director class that constructs an object using a builder interface. The builder interface defines methods for creating the parts of the product, and the director controls the order in which these methods are called.

Components

The Builder pattern consists of several key components:

+ **Product:** The complex object that is being constructed.

+ **Builder:** An interface that defines methods for creating the parts of the product.

+ **ConcreteBuilder:** A class that implements the Builder interface and provides specific implementations for the product's parts.

+ **Director:** A class that constructs the object using the Builder interface. It controls the construction process.

Problems Addressed

The Builder pattern addresses several common problems in software design:

+ **Complex Object Construction:** When an object requires numerous parameters, the constructor can become unwieldy and difficult to use.

+ **Immutability:** If an object is immutable, the Builder pattern allows for its construction without exposing its internal state during the process.

+ **Variability of Object Representation:** When different representations of an object are required, the Builder pattern facilitates this by allowing different builders to create variations of the product.

Example

Consider a scenario where we need to create a complex 'House' object that has multiple attributes such as 'walls', 'roof', 'windows', and 'doors'. Using the Builder pattern, we can construct a 'House' step by step.

```
class House {
    private String walls;
    private String roof\index{roof};
    private int\index{int} windows;
    private int\index{int} doors;

    // Constructor is private to enforce the use of the Builder
    private House(HouseBuilder builder) {
        this.walls = builder.walls;
        this.roof = builder.roof;
        this.windows = builder.windows;
        this.doors = builder.doors;
    }

    public static class HouseBuilder {
        private String walls;
        private String roof\index{roof};
```

```
        private int\index{int} windows;
        private int\index{int} doors;

        public HouseBuilder setWalls(String walls) {
            this.walls = walls;
            return\index{return} this;
        }

        public HouseBuilder setRoof(String roof) {
            this.roof = roof;
            return\index{return} this;
        }

        public HouseBuilder setWindows(int windows) {
            this.windows = windows;
            return\index{return} this;
        }

        public HouseBuilder setDoors(int doors) {
            this.doors = doors;
            return\index{return} this;
        }

        public House build() {
            return new House(this);
        }
    }
}
```

In this example, the 'HouseBuilder' class provides methods to set each attribute of the 'House' object. The 'build()' method finalizes the construction and returns the constructed 'House' object.

Usage

To use the Builder pattern, a client can create a 'HouseBuilder' instance and set the desired attributes before calling the 'build()' method:

```
House myHouse = new House.HouseBuilder()
```

```
.setWalls("Brick")
.setRoof("Tile")
.setWindows(10)
.setDoors(2)
.build();
```

This approach enhances code readability and maintainability, allowing for the creation of complex objects in a clear and concise manner.

Conclusion

The Builder pattern is a powerful design tool that simplifies the construction of complex objects. By separating the construction logic from the representation, it not only makes the code cleaner but also enhances flexibility and scalability. Whether you are constructing a simple object or a complex entity with multiple attributes, the Builder pattern is an invaluable addition to your design toolkit.

Structural Patterns

Adapter

The Adapter pattern is a structural design pattern that allows objects with incompatible interfaces to work together. It acts as a bridge between two incompatible interfaces, enabling communication and interaction in a seamless manner. This pattern is particularly useful when integrating new features into an existing system without altering the original codebase.

Theory

The Adapter pattern typically involves three main components:

- **Target Interface:** This defines the domain-specific interface that the client uses.

- **Adapter:** This is the class that implements the target interface and translates requests from the client to the adaptee.

- **Adaptee:** This is the existing class with an interface that is incompatible with the target interface but needs to be used.

The core idea is to create a wrapper (the Adapter) that allows the client to interact with the adaptee without needing to know the specifics of its implementation. This encapsulation promotes code reusability and flexibility.

Problems Addressed

The Adapter pattern addresses several common problems in software design:

+ **Incompatibility:** When integrating new components or systems, existing interfaces may not align with new requirements. The Adapter pattern resolves this by providing a compatible interface.

+ **Code Modification:** Modifying existing code can introduce bugs and affect system stability. The Adapter allows for new functionality without changing existing code, preserving system integrity.

+ **Separation of Concerns:** By decoupling the client from the adaptee, the Adapter pattern fosters a clean separation of concerns, making the system easier to understand and maintain.

Example

Consider a scenario where we have a legacy system that processes data in a specific format, but we need to integrate a new service that provides data in a different format. Here's how we can implement the Adapter pattern.

```
% Target interface
class DataProcessor {
public:
    virtual void processData() = 0;
};

% Adaptee class
class LegacyDataService {
public:
    void legacyProcess() {
        // Processing logic for legacy data
    }
};
```

```
% Adapter class
class LegacyDataAdapter : public DataProcessor {
private:
    LegacyDataService* legacyService;
public:
    LegacyDataAdapter(LegacyDataService* service) : legacyService(

    void processData() override {
        legacyService->legacyProcess();
    }
};
```

In this example:

+ **DataProcessor** is the target interface that the client expects.

+ **LegacyDataService** is the adaptee that has a method `legacyProcess()` which is not compatible with `DataProcessor`.

+ **LegacyDataAdapter** implements the `DataProcessor` interface and translates the `processData()` call to the `legacyProcess()` method of the adaptee.

To use the Adapter, the client code can remain unchanged:

```
DataProcessor* processor = new LegacyDataAdapter(new LegacyDataSer
processor->processData();  // Client calls the adapter
```

This allows the client to work with the legacy service without needing to modify its code.

Conclusion

The Adapter pattern is a powerful tool in a programmer's arsenal, enabling the integration of disparate systems and promoting code reuse. By encapsulating the complexities of interfacing with legacy or incompatible components, it allows developers to focus on higher-level design and functionality, ultimately leading to more robust and maintainable software systems.

Decorator

The Decorator pattern is a structural design pattern that allows behavior to be added to individual objects, either statically or dynamically, without affecting the behavior of other objects from the same class. This pattern is particularly useful when you want to add responsibilities to objects at runtime, enhancing their functionality while adhering to the Open/Closed Principle.

Theory

The core concept behind the Decorator pattern is that it allows for the dynamic composition of behaviors. Instead of using inheritance to extend functionality, which can lead to an explosion of subclasses, the Decorator pattern provides a flexible alternative.

The key components of the Decorator pattern are:

- **Component:** An interface or abstract class defining the behavior that can be dynamically added to concrete components.

- **Concrete Component:** A class that implements the Component interface. This is the object to which additional responsibilities can be attached.

- **Decorator:** A class that also implements the Component interface and contains a reference to a Component object. It delegates calls to the wrapped component, allowing it to add its own behavior before or after delegating.

- **Concrete Decorators:** These are classes that extend the Decorator class and add specific behaviors or responsibilities.

Problems Addressed

The Decorator pattern addresses several common problems in software design:

- **Class Explosion:** When using inheritance to add functionality, the number of subclasses can grow rapidly, leading to a complicated class hierarchy. Decorators allow for more manageable code by composing behaviors.

- **Flexibility:** It provides greater flexibility in adding and removing responsibilities at runtime, as opposed to compile-time inheritance.

- **Single Responsibility Principle:** By using decorators, you can keep classes focused on a single responsibility, while allowing for the dynamic addition of behaviors.

Example

Let's consider a simple example of a coffee shop where we want to add different toppings to a basic coffee.

```Java
\begin{lstlisting}[language=Java]
interface Coffee {
    String getDescription();
    double cost();
}

class SimpleCoffee implements Coffee {
    public String getDescription() {
        return ``Simple Coffee";
    }

    public double cost() {
        return\index{return} 2.00;
    }
}

abstract class CoffeeDecorator implements Coffee {
    protected Coffee decoratedCoffee\index{Coffee decoratedCoffee}

    public CoffeeDecorator(Coffee coffee) {
        this.decoratedCoffee = coffee;
    }

    public String getDescription() {
        return decoratedCoffee.getDescription();
    }

    public double cost() {
        return decoratedCoffee.cost();
    }
}

class MilkDecorator extends CoffeeDecorator {
    public MilkDecorator(Coffee coffee) {
```

```java
        super(coffee);
    }

    public String getDescription() {
        return decoratedCoffee.getDescription() + ``, Milk";
    }

    public double cost() {
        return decoratedCoffee.cost() + 0.50;
    }
}

class SugarDecorator extends CoffeeDecorator {
    public SugarDecorator(Coffee coffee) {
        super(coffee);
    }

    public String getDescription() {
        return decoratedCoffee.getDescription() + ``, Sugar";
    }

    public double cost() {
        return decoratedCoffee.cost() + 0.25;
    }
}

// Usage
public class CoffeeShop {
    public static void main(String[] args) {
        Coffee coffee = new SimpleCoffee();
        System.out.println(coffee.getDescription() + `` \$'' + cof

        coffee = new MilkDecorator(coffee);
        System.out.println(coffee.getDescription() + `` \$'' + cof

        coffee = new SugarDecorator(coffee);
        System.out.println(coffee.getDescription() + `` \$'' + cof
    }
}
```

```
\end{lstlisting}
```

In this example, we have a basic 'SimpleCoffee' class that implements the 'Coffee' interface. We then create an abstract 'CoffeeDecorator' class that also implements the 'Coffee' interface. The 'MilkDecorator' and 'SugarDecorator' classes extend 'CoffeeDecorator', adding their specific functionality.

When executed, the output will be:

```
Simple Coffee \$2.0
Simple Coffee, Milk \$2.5
Simple Coffee, Milk, Sugar \$2.75
```

This demonstrates how we can dynamically add responsibilities to the 'SimpleCoffee' object without modifying its class.

Conclusion

The Decorator pattern is a powerful tool in a programmer's arsenal, allowing for flexible and reusable code. By adhering to the principles of composition over inheritance, it enables developers to create complex functionalities without the pitfalls of a rigid class hierarchy. In the context of Erich Gamma's contributions to software design, the Decorator pattern exemplifies the innovative thinking that has shaped modern programming practices.

In summary, the Decorator pattern not only enhances the functionality of individual objects but also promotes a cleaner and more maintainable codebase. As such, it remains a vital pattern in software design, especially in scenarios where behavior needs to be extended dynamically.

Proxy

The Proxy design pattern is a structural pattern that provides an object representing another object. This pattern allows a surrogate or placeholder to control access to the original object, enabling various functionalities such as lazy initialization, access control, logging, and more.

Theory

In essence, the Proxy pattern introduces an intermediary between the client and the real subject. This intermediary, or proxy, can manage the instantiation of the real subject, control access to it, or even extend its functionality. The Proxy pattern is often used in scenarios where the cost of creating an object is high, or where the object is not immediately needed.

The Proxy pattern typically involves three components:

- **Subject**: An interface that defines the operations that can be performed on the real object.

- **Real Subject**: The actual object that the proxy represents. It contains the core functionality.

- **Proxy**: A class that implements the Subject interface and holds a reference to the Real Subject. It can perform additional operations before or after delegating calls to the Real Subject.

Problems Addressed

The Proxy pattern addresses several problems, including:

- **Resource Management**: When creating an object is expensive, a Proxy can delay its creation until it is absolutely necessary (Lazy Initialization).

- **Access Control**: Proxies can restrict access to certain methods or properties of the Real Subject, providing a layer of security.

- **Logging and Monitoring**: Proxies can log requests made to the Real Subject, which is useful for debugging or monitoring purposes.

- **Remote Access**: In distributed systems, a Proxy can act as a local representative for a remote object, managing communication and data transfer.

Example

Consider a scenario where we have a `Image` class that represents a large image file. Loading the image from disk can be resource-intensive, and we may want to delay this operation until the image is actually needed. Here's how we can implement the Proxy pattern:

```
class Image {
public:
    void display() {
        // Code to display the image
```

```cpp
    }
};

class ProxyImage {
private:
    Image* realImage;
    std::string\index{string} filename\index{filename};

public:
    ProxyImage(std::string filename) : filename(filename), realIma

    void display() {
        if (realImage == nullptr) {
            realImage = new Image(filename); // Lazy initializatio
        }
        realImage->display();
    }
};
```

In this example, the `ProxyImage` class serves as a Proxy for the `Image` class. The actual `Image` object is only instantiated when `display()` is called for the first time. This approach saves resources by avoiding unnecessary loading of the image.

Implementation Considerations

When implementing the Proxy pattern, consider the following:

- **Interface Consistency:** Ensure that the Proxy implements the same interface as the Real Subject to maintain consistency in client interactions.

- **Performance Overhead:** While Proxies can improve performance in some scenarios, they can also introduce overhead due to the additional layer of indirection. Evaluate the trade-offs based on the specific use case.

- **Thread Safety:** If the Proxy and Real Subject are accessed by multiple threads, ensure that proper synchronization mechanisms are in place to prevent race conditions.

Conclusion

The Proxy design pattern is a powerful tool in a programmer's arsenal, providing a flexible way to manage access to objects while adding functionality. By implementing a Proxy, developers can enhance resource management, control access, and introduce additional behaviors without modifying the original object. This pattern is particularly useful in scenarios involving resource-intensive objects or remote services, making it a staple in modern software architecture.

Composite

The Composite Pattern is a structural design pattern that allows you to compose objects into tree structures to represent part-whole hierarchies. This pattern treats individual objects and compositions of objects uniformly. The Composite Pattern is particularly useful when you need to work with tree structures, such as graphics rendering, file systems, or organizational structures.

Theory

The Composite Pattern is defined by the following key components:

- **Component:** An interface or abstract class that declares the common operations for both simple and composite objects.

- **Leaf:** A concrete class that implements the Component interface. It represents the end objects in the composition that do not have any children.

- **Composite:** A class that implements the Component interface and contains a collection of Leaf or Composite objects. It defines methods to add, remove, and access child components.

The essence of the Composite Pattern is to allow clients to treat individual objects and compositions uniformly. This makes it easier to work with complex tree structures without having to differentiate between the types of objects.

Structure

The structure of the Composite Pattern can be illustrated as follows:

In this diagram: - The `Component` defines the interface for objects in the composition. - The `Leaf` represents the individual objects in the composition. - The `Composite` holds the child components and implements the methods defined in the `Component` interface.

Problems Addressed

The Composite Pattern addresses several problems in software design:

* **Complexity Management**: It simplifies the client code by allowing clients to work with a uniform interface for both individual objects and compositions.

* **Hierarchical Structures**: It facilitates the creation and management of tree structures, enabling recursive operations on the hierarchy.

* **Extensibility**: New components can be added without altering existing code, adhering to the Open/Closed Principle.

Examples

Consider a graphical application where shapes can be grouped together. Using the Composite Pattern, we can define a hierarchy of shapes as follows:

```cpp
class Shape {
    public:
        virtual void draw() = 0; // Abstract method
};

class Circle : public Shape {
    public:
        void draw() {
            std::cout << ``Drawing a Circle'' << std::endl;
        }
};

class Rectangle : public Shape {
    public:
        void draw() {
            std::cout << ``Drawing a Rectangle'' << std::endl;
        }
};

class CompositeShape : public Shape {
    private:
        std::vector<Shape*> shapes; // Collection of child shapes
```

```
public:
    void add(Shape* shape) {
        shapes.push_back(shape);
    }

    void draw() {
        for (Shape* shape : shapes) {
            shape->draw(); // Delegates the draw call to chil
        }
    }
};
```

In this example, `Shape` is the component interface, while `Circle` and `Rectangle` are leaf nodes. The `CompositeShape` class can contain multiple shapes and delegates the drawing operation to its children.

Usage Scenarios

The Composite Pattern is widely used in scenarios such as:

- **Graphic Systems**: Where complex drawings can be composed of simple shapes.

- **File Systems**: Where directories can contain files and other directories.

- **UI Components**: Where complex interfaces can be composed of simple components like buttons, panels, and dialogs.

Conclusion

The Composite Pattern is a powerful tool in the software design arsenal, enabling developers to build flexible and maintainable systems that can represent complex hierarchies. By using this pattern, you can simplify the client code and enhance the extensibility of your applications. Whether you are designing a graphical application, a file system, or a user interface, the Composite Pattern provides a robust solution for managing part-whole relationships.

Behavioral Patterns

Observer

The Observer pattern is a behavioral design pattern that defines a one-to-many dependency between objects so that when one object changes state, all its dependents are notified and updated automatically. This pattern is particularly useful in scenarios where a change in one object necessitates updates in other objects, making it a cornerstone in event-driven programming and the implementation of reactive systems.

Theory

The Observer pattern consists of two main components: the **Subject** and the **Observer**. The Subject maintains a list of Observers that are interested in its state changes. When the state of the Subject changes, it notifies all registered Observers. This decouples the Subject from its Observers, allowing for flexibility and scalability in software design.

The relationship can be formally represented as follows:

$$\text{Subject} \longleftrightarrow \text{notifiesObservers} \tag{32}$$

Where: - The **Subject** has methods to attach and detach Observers. - The **Observer** interface defines the method that will be called to update the Observer.

Implementation

The implementation of the Observer pattern can be broken down into several key steps:

1. **Define the Observer Interface**: This interface will declare the update method that the Observers must implement.

```
class Observer {
    void update();
}
```

2. **Create the Subject Class**: This class will maintain a list of Observers and will provide methods to add, remove, and notify Observers.

```java
class Subject {
    private List<Observer> observers = new ArrayList<>();

    void attach(Observer observer) {
        observers.add(observer);
    }

    void detach(Observer observer) {
        observers.remove(observer);
    }

    void notifyObservers() {
        for (Observer observer : observers) {
            observer.update();
        }
    }
}
```

3. **Concrete Subject**: This class extends the Subject and maintains the state that Observers are interested in.

```java
class ConcreteSubject extends Subject {
    private int\index{int} state\index{state};

    public int getState() {
        return state;
    }

    public void setState(int state) {
        this.state = state;
        notifyObservers();
    }
}
```

4. **Concrete Observer**: This class implements the Observer interface and defines the update method to respond to changes in the Subject.

```java
class ConcreteObserver implements Observer {
```

```
        private ConcreteSubject subject\index{subject};

        public ConcreteObserver(ConcreteSubject subject) {
            this.subject = subject;
            subject.attach(this);
        }

        public void update() {
            System.out.println("State updated to: `` + subject.getS
        }
    }
```

Example

Let's consider a practical example of a weather station that uses the Observer pattern. The weather station (Subject) has temperature data that multiple display devices (Observers) need to be updated with.

```
class WeatherStation extends ConcreteSubject {
    public void changeTemperature(int newTemperature) {
        setState(newTemperature);
    }
}

class TemperatureDisplay implements Observer {
    private WeatherStation weatherStation;

    public TemperatureDisplay(WeatherStation weatherStation) {
        this.weatherStation = weatherStation;
        weatherStation.attach(this);
    }

    public void update() {
        System.out.println("Temperature Display: `` + weatherStati
    }
}
```

In this example, when the weather station's temperature changes, all registered displays will receive the update automatically:

```
WeatherStation weatherStation = new WeatherStation();
TemperatureDisplay display1 = new TemperatureDisplay(weatherStat:
TemperatureDisplay display2 = new TemperatureDisplay(weatherStat

weatherStation.changeTemperature(25); // Outputs: Temperature Dis
```

Problems and Considerations

While the Observer pattern provides significant benefits, it also introduces some challenges:

1. **Memory Leaks**: If Observers are not properly detached from the Subject, it can lead to memory leaks, as the Subject holds references to the Observers.

2. **Unpredictable Updates**: The order of notifications is not guaranteed. If multiple Observers are dependent on one another, this can lead to inconsistent states.

3. **Performance**: If a Subject has many Observers, notifying them can become a performance bottleneck, especially if the update logic is complex.

4. **Tight Coupling**: Although the pattern promotes loose coupling, changes in the Subject's state may still require knowledge of the Observers, leading to potential tight coupling.

In conclusion, the Observer pattern is a powerful tool in a programmer's arsenal, enabling dynamic and responsive systems. Its implementation can greatly enhance the modularity and flexibility of software applications, making it a vital concept in modern software engineering.

Strategy

The Strategy Pattern is a behavioral design pattern that enables an algorithm's behavior to be selected at runtime. It defines a family of algorithms, encapsulates each one, and makes them interchangeable. This pattern lets the algorithm vary independently from clients that use it. The Strategy Pattern is particularly useful when you have multiple ways to perform a task, and you want to select the appropriate method at runtime based on the specific context.

Theory

The core idea behind the Strategy Pattern is to separate the behavior of a class from its context. This is achieved through the use of interfaces or abstract classes that define the strategies. The client can then choose which strategy to use at runtime without needing to modify the class that uses the strategy.

$$\text{Context} \rightarrow \text{Strategy} \rightarrow \text{ConcreteStrategy} \qquad (33)$$

Where:

+ **Context** is the class that uses the strategy.

+ **Strategy** is the interface that defines the algorithm.

+ **ConcreteStrategy** is the implementation of the strategy.

Problems Addressed

The Strategy Pattern addresses several problems commonly encountered in software design:

+ **Code Duplication:** When multiple classes implement similar algorithms, the Strategy Pattern allows for code reuse by encapsulating the algorithms in separate strategy classes.

+ **Complexity in Context Classes:** By delegating the algorithmic behavior to separate strategy classes, the context class remains focused on its core responsibilities, leading to cleaner, more maintainable code.

+ **Runtime Flexibility:** The Strategy Pattern provides the ability to change the behavior of a class at runtime, allowing for greater flexibility and adaptability in the system.

Example

Consider a payment processing system that supports multiple payment methods, such as credit card, PayPal, and cryptocurrency. Instead of hardcoding the payment logic within the payment processing class, we can use the Strategy Pattern to encapsulate each payment method as a separate strategy.

```
interface PaymentStrategy {
    void pay(int amount);
}

class CreditCardPayment implements PaymentStrategy {
    public void pay(int amount) {
        System.out.println("Paid `` + amount + `` using Credit Car
```

```java
        }
}

class PayPalPayment implements PaymentStrategy {
    public void pay(int amount) {
        System.out.println("Paid `` + amount + `` using PayPal.")
    }
}

class CryptoPayment implements PaymentStrategy {
    public void pay(int amount) {
        System.out.println("Paid `` + amount + `` using Cryptocur
    }
}

class ShoppingCart {
    private PaymentStrategy paymentStrategy;

    public void setPaymentStrategy(PaymentStrategy paymentStrateg
        this.paymentStrategy = paymentStrategy;
    }

    public void checkout(int amount) {
        paymentStrategy.pay(amount);
    }
}
```

In this example, the ShoppingCart class can dynamically choose the payment method at runtime:

```java
ShoppingCart cart = new ShoppingCart();
cart.setPaymentStrategy(new CreditCardPayment());
cart.checkout(100); // Output: Paid 100 using Credit Card.

cart.setPaymentStrategy(new PayPalPayment());
cart.checkout(200); // Output: Paid 200 using PayPal.
```

Conclusion

The Strategy Pattern is a powerful tool in a programmer's toolkit, providing a way to manage algorithms flexibly and cleanly. By encapsulating algorithms and allowing them to be selected at runtime, this pattern not only promotes code reuse and separation of concerns but also enhances the maintainability and scalability of software systems. Its applicability extends across various domains, making it a cornerstone of effective software design.

Template Method

The Template Method pattern is a behavioral design pattern that defines the skeleton of an algorithm in a method, deferring some steps to subclasses. This pattern lets subclasses redefine certain steps of an algorithm without changing the algorithm's structure. The Template Method is particularly useful for code reuse and for managing variations in algorithms.

Theory

The Template Method pattern consists of two main components:

- **Abstract Class:** This class contains the template method, which defines the algorithm's structure. It also includes abstract methods that subclasses must implement.

- **Concrete Class:** These classes inherit from the abstract class and implement the abstract methods, providing specific behaviors.

The main advantage of the Template Method pattern is that it promotes code reuse and the inversion of control. By defining the core algorithm in the abstract class, you can ensure that the overall process remains consistent while allowing for flexible customization in subclasses.

Structure

The structure of the Template Method pattern can be illustrated as follows:

```
class AbstractClass {
    public final void templateMethod() {
        stepOne();
        stepTwo();
```

```
        stepThree();
    }

    protected abstract void stepOne();
    protected abstract void stepTwo();

    protected void stepThree() {
        // Default implementation (optional)
    }
}

class ConcreteClassA extends AbstractClass {
    protected void stepOne() {
        // Implementation for ConcreteClassA
    }

    protected void stepTwo() {
        // Implementation for ConcreteClassA
    }
}

class ConcreteClassB extends AbstractClass {
    protected void stepOne() {
        // Implementation for ConcreteClassB
    }

    protected void stepTwo() {
        // Implementation for ConcreteClassB
    }
}
```

Problems Addressed

The Template Method pattern addresses several common problems in software development:

+ **Code Duplication:** By centralizing the algorithm's structure in the abstract class, you avoid duplicating code across different implementations.

- Inconsistent Algorithm Behavior: The pattern enforces a consistent algorithm structure, ensuring that subclasses adhere to the defined steps.

- **Difficulty in Extending Algorithms:** By using the Template Method, you can easily extend or modify the algorithm by adding new subclasses or overriding existing methods.

Examples

To illustrate the Template Method pattern, consider a simple scenario involving data processing. Suppose we have an abstract class 'DataProcessor' that defines a template method for processing data.

```
abstract class DataProcessor {
    public final void processData() {
        readData();
        processData();
        saveData();
    }

    protected abstract void readData();
    protected abstract void processData();

    protected void saveData() {
        // Default implementation for saving data
    }
}

class CSVDataProcessor extends DataProcessor {
    protected void readData() {
        // Implementation for reading CSV data
    }

    protected void processData() {
        // Implementation for processing CSV data
    }
}

class XMLDataProcessor extends DataProcessor {
    protected void readData() {
```

```
        // Implementation for reading XML data
    }

    protected void processData() {
        // Implementation for processing XML data
    }
}
```

In this example, both 'CSVDataProcessor' and 'XMLDataProcessor' inherit from 'DataProcessor' and implement the specific steps for reading and processing their respective data formats. The 'saveData' method, which could be common across all processors, is provided with a default implementation in the abstract class.

Conclusion

The Template Method pattern is a powerful tool for designing flexible and reusable algorithms. By separating the algorithm's structure from its specific implementations, developers can create extensible systems that adhere to the principles of object-oriented design. This pattern is particularly beneficial in scenarios where the overall process remains constant, but the details vary based on specific requirements.

In summary, the Template Method pattern:

- Encourages code reuse and consistency.

- Simplifies the management of algorithm variations.

- Provides a clear structure for developers to follow when implementing new behaviors.

By understanding and applying the Template Method pattern, software developers can create robust and maintainable systems that stand the test of time.

Command

The Command pattern is a behavioral design pattern that encapsulates a request as an object, thereby allowing for parameterization of clients with queues, requests, and operations. This pattern is particularly useful in scenarios where operations need to be executed at a later time, undoable operations are required, or when operations need to be logged.

Theory

The Command pattern consists of four main components:

- **Command:** This interface declares a method for executing a command.

- **ConcreteCommand:** This class implements the Command interface and defines the binding between a receiver and an action. It invokes methods on the receiver to carry out the request.

- **Receiver:** This class knows how to perform the operations associated with carrying out a request. The receiver is the object that the command operates on.

- **Invoker:** This class asks the command to execute the request. It holds a command and can execute it at any time.

The key advantage of using the Command pattern is the separation of concerns, which allows for greater flexibility and extensibility in code. By encapsulating requests as objects, the Command pattern enables features such as queuing operations, logging them, and supporting undoable actions.

Problems Addressed

The Command pattern addresses several common problems in software design:

- **Decoupling Sender and Receiver:** The invoker does not need to know the details of how the command is executed. This decoupling allows for easier modifications and extensions.

- **Undo/Redo Functionality:** By maintaining a history of commands, the Command pattern can easily implement undo and redo functionality.

- **Parameterization of Objects:** Clients can be parameterized with different commands, allowing for dynamic behavior.

- **Logging Requests:** Commands can be logged for audit purposes, providing a history of operations performed.

Example

To illustrate the Command pattern, consider a simple text editor application where users can perform operations such as typing, deleting, and undoing actions.

```cpp
class Command {
    public:
        virtual void execute() = 0;
        virtual void undo() = 0;
};

class TextEditor {
    private:
        std::string\index{string} text\index{text};
    public:
        void append(const std::string\& newText) {
            text += newText;
        }

        void deleteLast(int length) {
            text.erase(text.size() - length);
        }

        std::string getText() {
            return text;
        }
};

class AppendCommand : public Command {
    private:
        TextEditor* editor;
        std::string\index{string} textToAppend;
    public:
        AppendCommand(TextEditor* editor, const std::string\& tex
            : editor(editor), textToAppend(text) {}

        void execute() override {
            editor->append(textToAppend);
        }
```

```
        void undo() override {
            editor->deleteLast(textToAppend.length());
        }
};

class Invoker {
    private:
        Command* command;
    public:
        void setCommand(Command* cmd) {
            command = cmd;
        }

        void executeCommand() {
            command->execute();
        }

        void undoCommand() {
            command->undo();
        }
};
```

In this example, the TextEditor class acts as the receiver, while AppendCommand is a concrete command that implements the command interface. The Invoker class allows the client to execute and undo commands without knowing the specifics of how these commands are implemented.

Usage Scenarios

The Command pattern is particularly useful in the following scenarios:

+ When you need to implement a queue of operations, allowing requests to be processed in a specific order.

+ When operations need to be reversible, such as in applications that support undo functionality.

+ When you want to log actions for audit trails or debugging purposes.

+ When you need to parameterize objects with different actions, enabling dynamic behavior.

Conclusion

The Command pattern is a powerful tool in the software developer's toolkit, providing a robust framework for managing operations in a decoupled and flexible manner. Its ability to encapsulate requests as objects not only enhances code maintainability but also opens the door to advanced features like undo/redo functionality and logging. By leveraging the Command pattern, developers can create more intuitive and user-friendly applications that respond elegantly to user actions.

Glossary

Key terms and concepts

Definitions and explanations

In this section, we will define key terms and concepts related to design patterns and software development. Understanding these definitions is crucial for grasping the significance of design patterns and their applications in programming.

Design Pattern

A design pattern is a general reusable solution to a commonly occurring problem within a given context in software design. It is not a finished design that can be transformed directly into code; rather, it is a description or template for how to solve a problem in various situations.

Example: The Singleton pattern ensures that a class has only one instance and provides a global point of access to it. This is particularly useful when exactly one object is needed to coordinate actions across the system.

Creational Patterns

Creational patterns deal with object creation mechanisms, trying to create objects in a manner suitable to the situation. These patterns increase flexibility and reuse of existing code.

Key Creational Patterns:

+ **Factory Method:** Defines an interface for creating an object but lets subclasses alter the type of objects that will be created.

+ **Abstract Factory:** Provides an interface for creating families of related or dependent objects without specifying their concrete classes.

- **Singleton:** Ensures a class has only one instance and provides a global point of access to it.

- **Builder:** Separates the construction of a complex object from its representation, allowing the same construction process to create different representations.

Structural Patterns

Structural patterns deal with object composition, creating relationships between objects to form larger structures. They help ensure that if one part of a system changes, the entire system doesn't need to do the same.

Key Structural Patterns:

- **Adapter:** Allows the interface of an existing class to be used as another interface. It acts as a bridge between two incompatible interfaces.

- **Decorator:** Adds new functionality to an existing object without altering its structure. This is achieved by creating a set of decorator classes that are used to wrap concrete components.

- **Proxy:** Provides a surrogate or placeholder for another object to control access to it.

- **Composite:** Composes objects into tree structures to represent part-whole hierarchies. It allows clients to treat individual objects and compositions uniformly.

Behavioral Patterns

Behavioral patterns focus on communication between objects, what goes on between objects and how they operate together. They help define how objects interact in a system.

Key Behavioral Patterns:

- **Observer:** Defines a one-to-many dependency between objects so that when one object changes state, all its dependents are notified and updated automatically.

- **Strategy:** Defines a family of algorithms, encapsulates each one, and makes them interchangeable. It lets the algorithm vary independently from clients that use it.

- **Template Method:** Defines the skeleton of an algorithm in the superclass but lets subclasses override specific steps of the algorithm without changing its structure.

- **Command:** Encapsulates a request as an object, thereby allowing for parameterization of clients with queues, requests, and operations.

Software Engineering

Software engineering is the systematic application of engineering approaches to software development in a methodical way. It encompasses various processes, methodologies, and practices to ensure the quality and efficiency of software products.

Key Concepts in Software Engineering:

- **Agile Development:** An iterative approach to software development that focuses on collaboration, customer feedback, and small, rapid releases.

- **Waterfall Model:** A sequential design process often used in software development processes, in which progress is seen as flowing steadily downwards (like a waterfall) through phases.

- **Version Control:** A system that records changes to files or sets of files over time so that specific versions can be recalled later.

Object-Oriented Programming (OOP)

Object-oriented programming is a programming paradigm based on the concept of "objects", which can contain data and code: data in the form of fields (often known as attributes or properties), and code in the form of procedures (often known as methods).

Key Principles of OOP:

- **Encapsulation:** The bundling of data with the methods that operate on that data, restricting direct access to some of the object's components.

- **Inheritance:** A mechanism in which one class can inherit the attributes and methods of another class, promoting code reuse.

- **Polymorphism:** The ability to present the same interface for different data types, allowing methods to do different things based on the object it is acting upon.

Software Architecture

Software architecture refers to the high-level structures of a software system and the discipline of creating such structures. It involves the set of structures needed to reason about the system, which comprises software elements, relations among them, and properties of both.

Key Concepts in Software Architecture:

- **Microservices:** An architectural style that structures an application as a collection of loosely coupled services, which implement business capabilities.

- **Monolithic Architecture:** A traditional model for building software applications in which all components of the application are interconnected and interdependent.

- **Service-Oriented Architecture (SOA):** A design pattern based on structured collections of services that communicate with each other, often using protocols such as HTTP or SOAP.

Testing and Quality Assurance

Testing and quality assurance are processes aimed at ensuring that software products meet specified requirements and are free of defects.

Key Testing Concepts:

- **Unit Testing:** A software testing method by which individual pieces of code are tested to determine if they are fit for use.

- **Integration Testing:** A phase in software testing in which individual software modules are combined and tested as a group.

- **System Testing:** The process of testing an integrated hardware and software system to verify that it meets specified requirements.

Version Control Systems

Version control systems are tools that help software teams manage changes to source code over time. They enable multiple developers to work on a project simultaneously without conflicting changes.

Key Version Control Systems:

- **Git:** A distributed version control system that allows multiple developers to work on a project simultaneously without interfering with each other.

- **Subversion (SVN):** A centralized version control system that allows developers to manage changes to files and directories over time.

- **Mercurial:** A distributed version control system known for its efficiency and scalability.

By understanding these definitions and concepts, readers can appreciate the intricacies of software development and the vital role that design patterns play in creating robust, maintainable, and efficient software systems.

Understanding the jargon of software development

In the realm of software development, a unique lexicon has emerged that can often bewilder newcomers and even seasoned professionals. This section aims to demystify some of the most common terms and phrases used in the industry, providing clarity and context to enhance understanding.

1. Algorithm

An algorithm is a well-defined sequence of steps or rules designed to solve a specific problem or perform a task. In programming, algorithms serve as the backbone of data processing and computation. For example, a sorting algorithm organizes a list of items in a particular order.

$$\text{Sorted List} = \text{Sort}(\text{Unsorted List}) \tag{34}$$

Common sorting algorithms include QuickSort, MergeSort, and Bubble Sort, each with its own efficiency and use cases.

2. API (Application Programming Interface)

An API is a set of rules and protocols for building and interacting with software applications. It defines the methods and data formats that applications can use to communicate with each other. For instance, a weather application may use an API to fetch real-time weather data from a remote server.

$$\text{Weather Data} = \text{API.Request}(\text{Endpoint}) \tag{35}$$

APIs facilitate the integration of different software systems, enabling them to work together seamlessly.

3. Framework

A framework is a pre-built collection of code that provides a foundation for developing software applications. It includes libraries, tools, and conventions that streamline the development process. For example, the Django framework simplifies web development in Python by offering built-in components for database management, authentication, and URL routing.

$$\text{Web Application} = \text{Django Framework} + \text{Custom Code} \qquad (36)$$

Using a framework can significantly reduce development time and improve code quality.

4. IDE (Integrated Development Environment)

An IDE is a software application that provides comprehensive facilities to programmers for software development. It typically includes a code editor, debugger, and build automation tools. Popular IDEs include Visual Studio, IntelliJ IDEA, and Eclipse.

$$\text{Project} = \text{IDE}(\text{Code Editor} + \text{Debugger} + \text{Compiler}) \qquad (37)$$

An IDE enhances productivity by integrating all necessary tools into a single interface.

5. Version Control

Version control is a system that records changes to files over time, allowing developers to track revisions and collaborate efficiently. Git is one of the most widely used version control systems. It enables developers to maintain a history of changes and manage different versions of their code.

$$\text{Repository} = \text{Version Control}(\text{Commits} + \text{Branches}) \qquad (38)$$

This system is essential for collaborative projects, as it prevents conflicts and allows for easy rollback to previous versions.

6. Bug

A bug is an error or flaw in software that produces incorrect or unexpected results. Bugs can arise from various sources, including coding mistakes, incorrect assumptions, or unforeseen interactions between components. Debugging is the process of identifying and fixing these issues.

$$\text{Fixed Code} = \text{Original Code} - \text{Bug} \qquad (39)$$

Effective debugging techniques are crucial for maintaining software quality.

7. Refactoring

Refactoring is the process of restructuring existing computer code without changing its external behavior. The goal is to improve the code's readability, reduce complexity, and enhance maintainability. This practice helps developers keep the codebase clean and efficient.

$$\text{Refactored Code} = \text{Original Code} + \text{Improved Structure} \qquad (40)$$

Regular refactoring can prevent technical debt and improve long-term project sustainability.

8. Agile Development

Agile development is a methodology that emphasizes iterative progress, collaboration, and flexibility in software development. Agile teams work in short cycles called sprints, allowing for rapid adaptation to changes in requirements or market conditions.

$$\text{Product Increment} = \text{Agile Sprint}(\text{User Stories} + \text{Feedback}) \qquad (41)$$

This approach promotes continuous improvement and customer satisfaction.

9. Deployment

Deployment refers to the process of delivering a completed application to users. It involves configuring the application to run in a production environment, ensuring that all components are correctly set up and functioning. Continuous deployment practices automate this process, allowing for frequent updates.

$$\text{Live Application} = \text{Deployment}(\text{Build} + \text{Environment Configuration}) \qquad (42)$$

Effective deployment strategies are essential for maintaining uptime and user satisfaction.

10. Scalability

Scalability is the capability of a system to handle a growing amount of work or its potential to accommodate growth. A scalable application can maintain performance levels as user demand increases. This can be achieved through vertical scaling (adding resources to a single node) or horizontal scaling (adding more nodes).

$$\text{Performance} = \text{Scalability}(\text{Load} + \text{Resources}) \tag{43}$$

Designing scalable systems is critical for long-term success in software development.

Conclusion

Understanding the jargon of software development is essential for effective communication within the field. Familiarity with these terms not only aids in grasping complex concepts but also fosters collaboration among developers, ultimately leading to more successful projects. As the industry continues to evolve, staying updated with the latest terminology will empower programmers to navigate their careers with confidence.

Index

9 781779 699879